GLOSS.
MARKETII

GLOSSARY OF
MARKETING TERMS

Norman A. Hart
MSc, MCam, DipM, FIPR

John Stapleton
DBA, DipM

Published on behalf of
the Institute of Marketing
and the CAM Foundation

HEINEMANN : LONDON

William Heinemann Ltd
15 Queen Street, Mayfair, London W1X 8BE

LONDON   MELBOURNE   TORONTO
JOHANNESBURG   AUCKLAND

First published 1977

434 91860 1

Printed in Great Britain by
Willmer Brothers Limited, Birkenhead

PREFACE

This work is an attempt to set down in one volume a complete range of marketing and associated terms, and to provide a short explanation of each. It may be that in many instances a descriptive, rather than definitive, explanation is given. This, for the most part, is because there have never existed universally accepted definitions; rather there has evolved a number of alternative interpretations, sometimes in direct conflict with one another.

In this Glossary, there are over 1500 terms which should be of value to people practising (and learning) the marketing functions, as well as those of their colleagues who have to be able to interpret and apply the bewildering jargon which is often presented. It must also be acknowledged that a number of terms which the authors felt merited inclusion are not strictly marketing terms, having been borrowed from other disciplines. However, in these cases, the terms have been selected upon the basis of frequent use and benefit in marketing operations and discussions.

In commissioning this book, the Institute of Marketing and the Communication, Advertising and Marketing Education (CAM) Foundation were well aware of the need for authenticity in what would be a pioneer work. Clearly, their sponsorship provides an implied seal of approval. Whilst the authors are in fact wholly responsible for the definitions, the views have been sought of all the leading trade and professional associations, and due regard has been paid to their frequently helpful comments.

The breadth of marketing and its related subjects has led to the inclusion of terms which cover a wide span of activities – research, management, export, packaging, advertising, raw materials, selling, public relations, law and so on. As a result, the terms when put into alphabetical order present an apparently confusing disarray.

Nevertheless, the intention is to provide a comprehensive range, conveniently located to meet the needs of the practising marketing man. The authors will certainly welcome any advice they may receive regarding content and coverage which could help to improve future editions.

Lastly, whilst we have both underestimated the magnitude of the task, we have derived a small pleasure from collecting together in a serious work, definitions of such odd-sounding but interesting terms as 'scamp', 'bleed', 'cold-calling', 'rears', 'shell scheme', 'knocking copy', and many others. It is hoped we have been able to make the useful contribution to the marketing vocabulary which is needed for the professional practice of marketing.

Norman Hart
John Stapleton

ACKNOWLEDGEMENTS

To the CAM Foundation and the Institute of Marketing for sponsoring this work, and to the British Industrial Marketing Association who initiated a glossary of marketing terms which was published privately under the authorship of Norman Hart in collaboration with Barbara Jackson.

Also our thanks to the dozens of people who have read the text and who have given many valuable comments and criticisms and in particular, to Heather Knight and Eileen Stapleton for once again unravelling a very complex manuscript and reproducing it in presentable typed form. We feel that one person has to be singled out for our especial gratitude; it is Ted Jenner, the Institute of Marketing's Director of Diploma Studies. Sharing our determination to achieve a high standard of authority and competence for the work, his advice and detailed comments have been invaluable at all stages.

Finally, thanks are above all due to our wives, not only for assisting throughout but especially bearing with us during the time taken in preparing this book.

N.A.H.
J.S.

DEDICATED WITH LOVE TO

EILEEN STAPLETON AND IRENE HART

A

ABC Audit Bureau of Circulation Ltd. An independent body supported by advertisers, advertising agencies, and media owners, which issues audited circulation figures for subscribing publications. Circulation figures lacking an ABC certificate may not be accurate.

Above-the-line advertising Any form of advertising for which a commission or fee is payable to a recognized advertising agency operating on behalf of its client(s). Usually press, television, radio, cinema, and posters. *See* Recognition. *See also* Below-the-line advertising.

Absorption Assignment of all costs, both fixed and variable, to goods and/or services provided.

Accelerated motion The apparently increased speed of movement obtained by projecting at normal speed a film that has been taken at less than normal speed when shooting.

Accelerator Relatively small change in demand for consumer goods resulting in a comparatively substantial change in demand for capital plant supplying these goods.

Accommodation bill Bill of Exchange signed by one person to accommodate another. By signing, the person concerned becomes a *guarantor* but receives no payment. He becomes liable if the acceptor fails to pay by the due date.

Account (1) In sales, an invoice. (2) In advertising, a client of an advertising or other agency, that is to say, an organization providing a service in consideration of which an income is derived; hence, the term account.

Account executive An executive in an advertising agency, or other such organization, responsible for the overall managing of a client's requirements. Sometimes known as Account Supervisor, Account Manager, or

Account Director, the different titles indicating degrees of responsibility.

Account group Sub-unit of an advertising agency, handling a group of clients or accounts. May be fully or partly selfcontained.

Acquisition Purchase of other companies, or manufacturing rights, as a way of expanding a company's activities or increasing its share of a market. Also may be a means of diversification without the risks accompanying the development of a new product; or countering competition with greater certainty than by mounting a direct campaign. *See* Diversification.

Across-the-network Schedule for a particular advertiser or programme series that specifies transmission simultaneously from all the transmitters constituting the network.

Activity sampling An observational technique, using discontinuous tests to estimate the incidence of any defined activity.

Adaptation Use of a basic idea, as in an advertisement, for other media, e.g. posters, point of sale, literature. Also to adapt an advertisement to another shape or size.

Added value Increase in value acquired by materials, components, or other commodities (including labour for example) as a result of any input, whether processing, assembling, handling, distributing, or any other marketing activity.

Address line Part of advertisement or promotional material which contains the address of the advertiser, or the address to which any inquiries should be sent. *See* Base line.

Ad hoc As and when required. Often refers to occasional market surveys.

Administered prices Price levels established by an

industry or group of companies within an industry, forming either a monopoly or a cartel. The practice of Resale Price Maintenance was stopped in the UK during 1963, rendering the 'administration of prices' illegal.

Ad valorem According to value. Usually applied to rates, taxes, duty and levies etc.

Advance freight Freight dues paid in advance. Enables an importer to take immediate delivery of shipment following endorsement of a bill of lading.

Advertisement department Part of a publishing or other organization in the communications business concerned with selling advertising space or time, either to an agency or direct to a client.

Advertisement manager Executive responsible for selling advertising on behalf of a publisher, television, radio station or display contractor. Also responsible for managing the advertisement department. Not to be confused with an Advert*ising* manager.

Advertiser Organization or person on whose behalf an advertisement appears, and who ultimately pays the bill.

Advertising Use of paid-for space in a publication, for instance, or time on television, radio or cinema, usually as a means of persuading people to take a particular course of action, or to reach a point of view. May also be taken to include posters and other outdoor advertising. *See* Above-the-line or Below-the-line advertising. *See also* Publicity.

Advertising agency Business organization set up to provide a service to clients ranging across booking advertising space, designing advertisements and producing them, devising media schedules, commissioning research, providing consultancy, and any associated marketing service. Origin was as agent of a publisher by whom a commission was payable. This system of remuneration still survives in the case of most advertising agencies.

Advertising commission   *See* Media commission. *See also* Agency commission.

Advertising manager Executive responsible for planning and implementing his company's advertising, also for managing the advertising department. Alternatively, may be known as Publicity manager, Sales promotion manager, Marketing services manager.

Advertising medium   Vehicle of communication which provides for some form of advertising, e.g. the press, television, radio and transport services. Alternatively, a communication channel designed specifically for the purpose of advertising, e.g. direct mail, exhibition, poster site, and some printed publications, e.g. catalogues.

Advertising rates   Basic charges made by advertising media for use of their services or facilities. *See* Rate card.

Advertising regulations Conditions imposed upon advertising by media owners, trade associations, or government. *See* Voluntary controls.

Advertising schedule Programme of planned advertisement insertions, showing detailed costs, timing, nature of media and the bookings to be reserved. *See* Media schedule.

Advertising Standards Authority   *See* ASA.

Advertising strategy   The overall plan of an advertising campaign. *See* Marketing strategy.

Aerosol Pressurized canister containing a liquid (or cream) which is ejected, usually in the form of a vapour, on the operation of a valve connected to a press button.

Affreightment, Contracts of Contracts for the carriage of goods by sea. Standard contracts are shown in bills of lading.

After date   Date of payment after that shown on a bill of lading.

After-sales service Service of carrying out repairs, maintenance and the supply of advice or spares after a sale has been transacted; also with a view to further sales. The provision of the service is usually essential to the sale of the product.

After sight A bill of exchange drawn after sight, becomes payable after acceptance, fixing a date of acceptance from acceptor.

Against all risks Term used in marine insurance meaning insured against all generally accepted risks.

Agency bills Bills of exchange drawn on and accepted by the UK branches of foreign banks, usually in London.

Agency commission *See* Media commission.

Agent (1) Person or organization with express or implied authority to act for another (the principal) in order to establish a contractual relationship between the principal and any third party. Also can act as legal representative. Advertising agencies are an important exception to this role, acting as principals for the services they purchase on behalf of their clients. (2) Term may be used in a general sense indicating the person or organization representing another.

Agent's lien Where the agent legally possesses goods still owned by its principal, it is said to have a lien for monies due from the principal.

Agent's torts Principal is jointly and severally liable for his agent's torts where the agent has been acting for him in the normal course of its agency or upon the instructions of the principal. An advertising agency is an exception.

Aggregate demand Expression of total demand for goods and services within a national economy, usually divided into consumer, industrial, public purchases and exports.

AIDA A mnemonic for Attention, Interest, Desire, Action, denoting the progressive steps of customer reaction in the process of making a sale. Dates from the late 19th century.

Aided recall Prompting respondents by inducing

association of ideas to help recall, particularly of television or cinema viewing. *See* Recall.

Air date   Normally refers to date of first transmission of a commercial or campaign via a broadcasting service.

Air time   Amount of time devoted or allocated to an advertisement on radio or television. May also refer to actual time of transmission.

Airway bill   May also be known as Air consignment note. Is used as a contract of carriage by air.

Algorithm   Rule for the solution of a problem in a finite number of steps, e.g. a full statement of an arithmetical procedure for evaluating Sin X to a stated precision (BS 3527).

Allonge   Attachment to a bill of lading allowing for the inclusion of extra endorsement.

Amongst matter   Position of an advertisement, where it is situated amongst editorial material.

Amortization   Accounting procedure for extinguishing initial investment in new product launch over a period of years. Also relates to depreciation of plant and equipment.

Analysis   Resolution into simple elements, e.g. summary of data into tabulated form. May take the form of a chart or diagram.

Animation   Movement added to static objects, especially in relation to cartoons.

Annuals   Periodicals which are published once a year, usually in the form of reference books.

Anonymous product testing   Tests in which different basic products are all presented in a common anonymous form, e.g. a plain pack. This complements the Pseudo product test in evaluating a consumer's ability to perceive intrinsic product differences.

Answer print   The first print of an edited colour film.

Appreciation   (1) Increase in value of asset, e.g.

following excess of demand over supply. (2) Summing up or appraisal of a situation or problem.

Appropriation   Used in advertising to refer to the total sum of money set aside for all parts of the advertising mix. Equally, there can be appropriations for other parts of marketing or general business activity. Sometimes referred to as Advertising budget.

Artwork   Pictorial or illustrative part of an advertisement, or publication, in its finished form ready for blockmaking or production, e.g. a retouched and masked photograph.

ASA   Advertising Standards Authority. An independent body set up and paid for by the advertising industry to ensure that its system of self-regulation works in the public interest. The Authority has an independent chairman. Its members are appointed by him to serve as individuals and not as representatives of any section or interest. Half of its members must be from outside advertising. The Authority maintains close contact with central and local government departments, consumer organizations, and trade associations and deals with complaints received through them or direct from the public.

Atmosphere   Qualitative or subjective value of a medium or publication for advertising purposes.

Atomistic evaluation   Evaluation of specific elements or steps in advertising, particularly using indices of advertising effectiveness. *See* Holistic evaluation.

Attention value   Extent to which an advertisement can secure the initial attention of a reader, sometimes expressed in quantitative form in Starch or other page-traffic studies. *See* Starch ratings.

Attitude research   An investigation, often by personal interview or group discussion, into the attitude of people towards an organization or its products.

Audience   Group of people exposed to any of the media,

but more usually associated with television, radio, or cinema. Audience is a passive word and does not necessarily imply 'attention' to an advertisement.

Audience composition Classification of audiences by particular characteristics, usually demographic.

Audience data Information relating to size and/or nature of an audience.

Audience flow Gain or loss of audience during a programme.

Audience research *See* Media research.

Audiovisual Any form or combination of visual (ciné film, transparency or video) and sound (record, tape, cassette, optical or magnetic sound track).

Audiovisual sales aids Equipment incorporating facilities for communicating by sight and sound, used by salesmen to simulate an actual demonstration.

Audit Formal examination of accounts or management resources.

Average Usual or normal; most often refers to 'mean' or arithmetic average, the formula for which is:

$$m = \frac{x_1 + x_2 + x_3 \dots x_n}{n}$$

where 'm' is the mean. The mean is unfortunately not always representative of each item in a series and, in such cases, other forms of average, such as the mode or median may be used.

Average cost pricing Pricing policy where an average price is established over a product range based on average cost.

Average frequency Average opportunities to see a commercial announcement among those who are reached at all, i.e. gross reach divided by net reach.

Average propensity to consume That part of national

income devoted, on average, by the nation's individuals to consumption of goods and services.

Average revenue   Total revenue divided by number of units sold.

B

Back cover   In advertising, the back cover of a magazine usually available at premium rates for advertising. Special rates apply to both inside and outside back covers. *See* Front cover.

Back freight   Additional charges payable due to freight not being collected within a reasonable time at the port of discharge. Often includes master handling goods at owner's expense and may include transferring goods to another port. May refer to charges for goods to consignor.

Background   (1) Secondary information relating to a marketing campaign. (2) Remoter part of an illustration or advertisement layout. (3) Sound effect or musical strain in a broadcast or film.

Backed note   An authority, endorsed by broker, to master of ship arranging the loading of goods for shipment.

Back-to-back credit   Credit provided to a buyer by finance house acting as contact between foreign buyers and sellers, particularly where the seller does not disclose identity. The terms embodied in the credit reflect the terms of the original sale.

Bad debts   Accounts going out of business and still owing money to suppliers. Also an item in financial accounts referring to actual amount of monies so lost, or written off.

Bag   Open ended container for wrapping goods usually at the point of sale. Made from paper or plastic, and sometimes including paperboard for added protection. Often bearing distinctive printing indicating origin, and advertising goods or services.

Balance of payments Details of credit and debit transactions of one country against all foreign countries and international institutions. Government control over balance of payments usually affects international marketing policies.

Balance of trade Nation's balance of payments for visibles on current account. *See* Invisible Exports.

Banded pack Special offer combining two related or unrelated products in one integral unit.

Banner Relating to an advertisement headline stretching across open space. Also large board or piece of fabric held or towed aloft bearing some slogan or symbol. Towed banners are illegal in UK.

Bar chart Illustration of data using bars or columns. Also known as a histogram.

Bargain (1) To negotiate for terms. (2) An offer providing unusual value, e.g. a reduction in price. The benefits may be largely illusory but are found to have a motivating influence.

Base line Part of an advertisement or promotional material, usually containing address, company name, logotype and maybe a slogan, situated at foot of page; often conforms to common house style. *See* Address line.

Basing-point pricing system Pricing system which ensures that final selling prices in an industry are identical irrespective of the location or freight charges involved. In calculations each plant is given a 'base' price and a variable charge per mile.

Basket Container made from various materials including cane, wood or paperboard, and having a carrying handle, used in horticulture mainly for tomatoes and soft fruit but also, in wire, used in self-service stores for collection of merchandise by customers.

Battered letter Typeface which has been damaged or is in some way faulty; shows up in printing as an indistinct letter.

Bayes Theorem (Bayesian Theorem) Recently acquired sample information combined with prior personal probabilities, so producing revised probabilities in order to embark on new courses of action which may then, repeatedly, be subjected to further inputs of information and revised. It is close to the process of elimination with the use of probability theory.

Behavioural research Research into human behaviour, singly or in groups, particularly in connection with consuming or buying habits but also concerned with wider aspects of social and organizational conduct.

Below-the-line advertising Advertising activities which do not normally make provision for a commission to be payable to an advertising agency. These include direct mail, exhibitions, demonstrations, point-of-sale material. *See* Sales promotion with which it is often wrongly confused. *See also* Above-the-line advertising.

Bias Statistical term referring to errors in sample survey results which may be due to the use of an unrepresentative sample but also to undue influence upon response by the agency conducting the survey or a combination of such causes.

Bidding theory Quantification of purchasing determinants and the application of probability theory to arrive at a pricing policy; the numerical expression of relevant factors and their measured likelihood of acceptance at different price levels.

Bill (1) Invoice. (2) Short for billboard – a placard or poster in outdoor advertising. (3) Announcement listing persons in a broadcast programme.

Billing Total value of business handled by an advertising agency in a given period. Gross turnover.

Bill of entry Document showing final clearance of imported goods by Customs officers.

Bill of exchange Unconditional order in writing, addressed by one person to another, signed by the person giving it, requiring the person to whom it is addressed to pay on demand, or at a fixed or determinable future time, a certain sum in money to, or to the order of, a specified person, or to bearer.

Bill of lading Shipping document used as consignment note, indicating contractual terms and the parties to the contract. There are normally three copies (1) retained by seller; (2) held by master of ship; and (3) sent to buyer of goods. It is often presented with a bill of exchange and may give good title to goods.

Bill of sale Document indicating transfer of title, although possession usually remains with the transferer. Used to raise money on loan. Similar to Building Society mortgage.

Bill of sale (absolute) Document indicating transfer of title and possession, and witnessed by a solicitor.

Bill of sale (conditional) Document indicating transfer of title but where transferer reserves the right to retake title upon fulfilment of specific conditions.

Bill of sight Used by an importer for declaration on goods where full details of a particular consignment may be uncertain. After inspection by Customs the entry details are 'perfected'.

Bill of sufference An authority to coastal vessels to carry dutiable goods between ports with bonded warehouses.

Binary (1) Of, or appearing to, two (BS 3527). (2) Variable which can have one of two values only (0 or 1). It replaces the normal counting system of 1, 2, 3, 4, 5 . . . n, by the values of 0 and 1 only. The basis for rapid computing in electronic data processing systems.

Bingo card Enquiry card bound into a magazine and containing matrix of numbers or letters which correlate with similar keys in advertisements or editorial items. Facilitates reader enquiries and is usually prepaid for return to publisher. May also be referred to as readers' enquiry card.

Blanket coverage Advertising without prior selection of specific target audience.

Bleed Advertisement or printed page which utilizes the entire page area, i.e. print extends beyond the margin to the edge of the page.

Blink-meter Used in advertising research to measure the frequency of a person's blinking, so giving indications of interest or arousal.

Blister pack Sheet of transparent plastic, moulded into the form of a 'blister' and laminated on to a backing sheet. This enclosure might then contain a quantity of small units, like screws or drawing pins, or just one item, e.g. an electric switch.

Block Plate of metal, rubber or plastic engraved, moulded, or cast for printing purposes (other than body type), e.g. of photographs or drawings.

Block pull Carefully printed proof from a block to enable the accuracy and quality of reproduction to be checked before printing order is executed.

Blow-up Considerable enlargement of photograph or other illustration.

Board Frequently used in reference to the Board of Management of a firm or other organisation. *See* Paperboard and Fibreboard.

Body copy Main copy in advertisement, as opposed to headlines or illustration.

Body matter (or type) Small type which forms the bulk of the text in an advertisement, or indeed any piece of printed material.

Bold face Typeface in printing which is particularly heavy so that it stands out from the other printed matter. Used especially for titles or headings requiring prominent display.

Bona fide In good faith. Most often used in the law of contract. Sometimes used to indicate genuine travellers, e.g. in Scotland, where licensing laws are more tolerant to the needs of the traveller.

Bonded goods Imported goods on which duty has not been paid. They are held in a bonded warehouse, e.g. supervised by a Customs and Excise official, awaiting payment of duty or for re-export or for use in goods due to be re-exported. Sold only to those going abroad at duty-free shops.

Bonding of salesmen Buying indemnity against possible loss arising from negligence or dishonesty through employment of salesmen.

Bonus/extra sized packs Larger pack, or pack with an additional smaller package of the same product but sold at the price usual for a standard pack.

Bonus payment An incentive payment to salesmen for above-the-norm achievement; often *ex gratia* rather than contractual.

Booklet Small book containing up to fifty or so pages. *See* Brochure.

Boolean operation An operation depending on the application of the rules of Boolean algebra. By extension, any operation in which the operands and results take either one or two values or states, i.e. any logical operation on single binary digits (BS 3527).

Booth Exhibition stand. *See* Shell scheme.

Born salesmen Sales or other personnel attributed with

natural qualities that result in superior selling achievement.

Bottle Narrow necked container, usually of glass, stoneware or plastics (BS 3130). The latter may be rigid, e.g. containing carbonated drinks, or pliable, e.g. for washing-up liquids, where hand pressure assists dispensing of contents.

Box Rigid container, completely formed at the point of manufacture, constructed of cardboard (strawboard or chipboard) and often covered with decorative paper, e.g. gift boxes, quality chocolate boxes. Also may be made from rigid plastics.

BRAD British Rate and Data. A detailed guide to media buyers.

Brainstorming An intensive group discussion to stimulate creative ideas and to solve business problems ranging from new product concepts to improved sales performance, brand names to co-operative strategies, advertising slogans to PR events. The essence of a brainstorming session is that no idea, no matter how apparently irrelevant, should be discarded without adequate consideration and debate, the intention being to repel normal inhibitions and stimulate every kind of suggestion.

Brand Established product name, wholly of a proprietary nature, and usually listed within the Register of Patents.

Brand awareness Extent to which a brand or brand name is recognized by potential buyers, and correctly associated with the particular product in question.

Branded goods Goods identified with a proprietary name, normally prepacked by the manufacturer, for promotional, security or trading purposes. Branded goods offer some protection to the retailer or the distributor under the 1893 Sale of Goods Act, the Trade Descriptions

Acts, 1968 and 1972, and the Supply of Goods (Implied Terms) Act, 1973.

Brand image *See* Image.

Brand leader Product which holds the greatest single share of a market.

Brand loyalty Active support by consumers in continuing consumption of a particular brand in the face of competition by other branded substitutes. Such loyalty is often subjective or subconscious.

Brand manager Executive responsible for the overall marketing, and particularly promotion, of a specific brand. Job function ranges from a co-ordination role to one in which profit objectives are built in. Sometimes titled product manager, especially in USA.

Breadboard Early form of prototype in which the performance of a product is reproduced but without the associated appearance or other characteristics. Derives from electrical or engineering products in which components are laid out on a board, thus facilitating changes in order to obtain optimum performance.

Breakdown Detailed assembly of data within defined categories. An advertising breakdown, for instance, would show the nature, medium and cost of each item within the campaign.

Breakeven Point at which any commercial venture becomes financially viable, i.e. when total expenditure is exactly matched by income, and therefore the point after which a profit begins to be made. This is of particular importance in the launching of a new product where a certain risk investment is necessary; therefore forecasts must be projected before proceeding, as to the circumstances and time within which the breakeven point will be reached. This provides both the information required for policy decisions but also a yardstick against which performance can be measured progressively. Hence the expression 'payback period' to denote time to elapse before all investment costs are recovered and profit will subsequently be generated.

Breakeven analysis Examination of relationships between sales revenue, fixed costs, and variable costs to determine the most profitable level of output or the most profitable product mix.

Breakeven point Point at which sales revenue covers all expenditure and no profit or loss is being made.

Brief Summary of facts, objectives and instructions relating to the requirements for the creation of a campaign, an advertisement, or any other element of a marketing operation.

British Export Board (BEB) Organization set up to replace the BNEC in 1971, and subsequently renamed the British Overseas Trade Board. *See* BNEC.

British Export Houses Association Association formed by the British Export House and Forwarding Agents to provide advice to British exporters.

British National Exports Council (BNEC) Organization set up to organize and direct the promotional activities of British export companies. Was replaced in 1971 by the British Export Board, subsequently renamed British Overseas Trade Board. *See* BEB.

British Road Services (BRS) Part of the publicly-owned National Freight Corporation. It is concerned with general haulage, operating a national network of lorries, bolster vehicles, bulk carriers, containers, low loaders, specialized lorries. It also controls British Road Services Parcels Ltd., a specialized parcel distribution service.

British Standards Institution Operating under a Royal charter, the Institution is government assisted. It is an independent body promoting the co-operation of both users and producers in the improvement, standardization and simplification of designs, products, and industrial materials in order to eliminate production of an excessive variety of patterns and designs intended to serve one purpose. Furthermore, BSI sets standards of quality and dimensions by specification and registers and licences standards of all descriptions. It also operates THE (Technical Help for Exporters), a body used to provide technical advice, guidance and information on foreign standards and competitive performances.

British Transport Docks Board Publicly-owned profit-making authority controlling the operation of most ports of England, Scotland and Wales. Formed by the Transport Act, 1962.

British Waterways Board Publicly-owned profit-making authority governing the system of canals, rivers and lochs used for commerce and pleasure.

Broadsheet (1) Printed promotional material usually with one or two folds, but opening up into a relatively large sheet. (2) Term referring to newspapers other than tabloids.

Brochure Stitched booklet, usually having eight or more pages, often with a prestige connotation. *See* Booklet.

Broker Agent who does not physically handle the goods with which he deals, nor having control over the terms involved in a contract. He may represent either a buyer or a seller.

Budget Estimate of future sources of income and expenditure including statement of intentions within a given period of time. Can relate to individual parts of the marketing mix, when it may include expenses only, or to the total marketing operation.

Budgetary control Methodical monitoring of planned income and expenditure by issuing sales targets, placing orders and authorizing payments within the context of a previously approved and detailed budget. Provision is made for continuous feedback which relates to all financial commitments and projected surpluses or over-expenditures.

Built-in obsolescence   Technique used to increase the need for replacement for products in an effort to maintain continuous high volume of output and sales.

Built-in stabilizers   Automatic buffers against violent fluctuations in the economy, reacting without related government intervention at any one time. Sometimes manipulated by Government to achieve desired effects on national economy.

Bulk cargo   Cargo of one commodity on board ship, sometimes as loose storage in hold.

Bulletin   (1) Brief, periodically issued, mailing or announcement. (2) Painted outdoor sign or display.

Bulletin board   (1) Poster, illuminated outdoor sign, or transparency, size forty-eight sheet or even larger. Often found in city centres or on trunk roads. (2) Notice board.

Bus side   Space on the side of a bus, available for advertising. Usually 17 ft 6 ins long by 1 ft 9½ ins deep.

Buyer   (1) Person responsible for making a final purchasing decision. (2) Executive in a company heading up the overall purchasing function. (3) Department head in a department store.

Buyers' market   Market situation in which excess manufacturing capacity and over-supply of a commodity puts buyers in strong negotiating position as the result of an imbalance between supply and demand. Particularly affects movement of prices for seasonal goods.

Buying motives   All those factors within a person or organization which combine to create a desire to purchase. Such factors are usually complex and comprise logical criteria like price, quality, delivery; but also highly subjective considerations, often difficult to locate, let alone

27

measure, such as prestige, brand image, colour, shape and packaging.

Buying signals Indirect indications of a prospect's growing interest in the product being presented.

Buying syndicates Collective negotiating and buying group. *See* Co-operative.

By-line Reporter's name printed above his story.

By-product Product, commodity, or service which becomes available as a result of production of some primary product.

C

Call analysis Study of salesmen's customer calling patterns.

Call frequency Frequency with which salesmen visit or contact customers. Distinguished from conventional journey cycle by customer categorizing into groups of varying priority.

Call frequency schedule Salesman's journey plan.

Calling cycle (Journey cycle) Average period between calls on a given customer.

Call rate Number of personal contacts made with customers or prospects within a given period of time. *See* Journey planning.

Campaign Organized course of action, planned carefully to achieve predefined objectives. Can relate to advertising, sales, public relations, or any part of the promotional mix.

Can Diminutive of canister. A metal container, usually of tin-coated mild steel or aluminium, for containing, preserving or dispensing liquids or solids, especially foodstuffs. Hence, colloquial form is 'tin'. Opened except in the case of aerosols by a metal-cutting tool.

Canvass (1) To interview a selected group either for research purposes or within a selling procedure. (2) Used in research to indicate coverage of an entire population rather than just a sample. Synonymous in this sense to polling or conducting a census. (3) In form of 'cold' canvass, reference is made to salesman calls on prospects not previously contacted.

Canvasser Sales representative or selling agent calling direct on users or consumers. Cold canvassing is the term used to describe a salesman's uninvited (often the first) call on a prospect.

Capital Monetary measure of assets employed in a business, hence return on capital (ROC). *See* Yield.

Capital goods Goods, usually for industry or commerce, which are likely to remain permanent fixtures or to be used continuously for a long period of time, e.g. plant and machinery. Contrary term is consumer goods, those entirely consumed shortly after purchase, e.g. soap, foodstuffs, oil.

Captain's entry Details provided by the master of a ship when requesting permission to unload.

Caption Short description relating to an illustration or diagram.

Captive audience Audience which, by virtue of its particular situation, is likely to be exposed to an advertising message *in toto*, e.g. a cinema or conference audience.

Captive market Group of purchasers who are obliged to buy a particular product due to some special circumstances, either where there is no other source of supply or where the supplier is the owner of the buyer's company.

Cardboard Popular term for paperboard.

Career salesman Sales personnel choosing selling as a

career rather than as a step in the promotional ladder.

Carnet International Customs document allowing temporary duty-free import of certain goods into specified countries; normally used for the import of sales promotional samples of no commercial value or for works of art or capital equipment, etc. for temporary use, e.g. for exhibition purposes.

Cartel (Kartel) Organization of a number of firms operating in one market intending to minimize competition. May take the form of 'bulk agreements' as used between the suppliers of post office exchange equipment; outstanding orders are shared out between the participating companies. Under progressive attack from EEC Common Market institutions.

Carton Strictly a folding carton constructed from paperboard, 'set-up' or closed by an adhesive and/or by interlocking of end or side flaps. Most commonly made out of a white-lined board which is printed. Can contain one or a number of units, or dry goods such as powder. Sometimes wrongly used to describe a fibreboard case.

Case *See* Fibreboard case. *See also* Packing case.

Case history Document giving facts about a campaign.

Case study Case history produced in such a way as to facilitate study/learning, e.g. final solution is omitted to allow student to formulate his own.

Cash and carry wholesalers Wholesale supermarket frequented by small retailers or caterers following frequent mailings by wholesalers.

Catalogue Publication containing descriptions or details of a number or range of products.

Caveat emptor Legal expression meaning 'let the buyer beware'. Has almost ceased to apply following the Trade Descriptions Acts, 1968 and 1972 and the Supply of Goods (Implied Terms) Act, 1973. The original assumption implied that a person was legally obliged to exercise his own commonsense in buying and would not obtain sympathy from the law if he failed to protect himself against deception.

Census Study of an entire population – a government census of population is usually carried out in the UK every ten years. Other censuses, e.g. of production and distribution, are also periodically taken in UK.

Census sample Apparently contradictory term but meaning a sample drawn from compiled census data.

Central Office of Information (COI) Production centre of the UK Government world-wide publicity network, available to the British exporter. It has nine regional offices in England, Scotland, Wales and Northern Ireland. The COI has six divisions each specializing in some craft and production service.

Centre for Inter-Firm Comparison Organization established in 1959 by the British Institute of Management and the British Productivity Council. It collects and distributes confidential information to participating members on their operating performances as compared to the average, and suggests reasons for any apparent deficiencies.

Certificate of origin Used to identify source of goods or materials. Useful for economic trading or political reasons, particularly where some privilege is granted in respect of certain producers or where restriction upon movement of goods has been imposed.

Chain stores Group of outlets, under single ownership, each offering a wide variety of merchandise according to local demand.

Channel of communication Any particular link between a communicator, e.g. an advertiser, and a receiver, e.g. potential customer. *See* Medium.

31

Channel of distribution   Specific means of channelling goods from their point of origin to their point of sale or consumption, e.g. wholesale to retail distribution or manufacturer to mail order concern.

Charge accounts   Credit facilities offered by stores to established customers making periodic payments.

Check list   Comprehensive categorization of actions to be taken in order to achieve a given effect with maximum efficiency.

Check out   Cash till at exit(s) of self-service stores and supermarkets where payment is made for goods.

Chi-squared   Statistical test to check whether and in what ways distributions of data differ from each other.

Circular   Piece of printed matter distributed, or circularized, to a defined group of people.

Circulation   Total number of distributed (subscribed or free) copies of a periodical or publication. *See* Readership.

Classified advertising   Grouping together into categories or classifications of advertising usually comprising small type-set or semi-display advertisements, e.g. situations vacant, properties required or for sale.

Clean bill of lading   Bill of lading without superimposed clauses or endorsement expressly declaring some defective condition of the goods on consignment.

Client   Person or organization, for whom a service is performed, such as advertising, market research or public relations. Sometimes used to refer to a customer.

Clip   (1) Shot or sequence of shots cut or clipped from a complete film. (2) Fastener for retaining connected documentation on movements or transactions.

Clipping   *See* Press cutting.

Clipping service   An agency which will extract relevant news items or advertisements concerning a product or company in return for a monetary consideration.

Closed circuit Transmitting pictures to a television receiver by wire instead of radio waves. Alternatively, using a TV camera to record events on videotape which can then be used to reproduce the record on suitable TV receivers.

Closing prices Price of a commodity or a company's shares in the market at the end of a day's trading.

Closing techniques Variations of method in soliciting buyer action.

Closing the sale Salesman technique in requesting his order from a buyer (and securing it).

Closure Means by which a pack is closed up, e.g. the top to a bottle, the cap to a can.

Cluster analysis Grouping attitudes by tendency to agree. Used in research to associate slightly different attitudes that, in general, have a tendency to agree.

Cluster sampling Sample units devised in local groups, often chosen geographically to reduce interview travelling costs.

Coarse screen Printing block having larger than usual screen to facilitate its use on lower quality paper, e.g. newsprint.

Cobweb theorem Analysis of supply and demand situation where supply is a reflection of demand at an earlier time and has, therefore, little relevance to current demand levels. Applies where short-term production capacity is fixed or dependent on seasonal patterns.

Codes of practice Laid down conditions under which business should be conducted in a particular area of activity. In marketing, best known perhaps is Code of Advertising Practice (CAP) but Market Research Society and Institute of Marketing also publish codes. Similar codes govern practice in sales promotion (issued by International Chambers of Commerce).

33

Coding (1) Keying of an advertisement to enable the origin of an enquiry to be traced. (2) Use of numbers or letters in a questionnaire against specific questions in order to facilitate analysis.

Cognitive dissonance State of mental conflict caused by taking an action which is in direct opposition to a particular belief or attitude. In marketing, an example would be pre or postpurchase anxiety as to the advisability of a particular choice, usually for more expensive goods.

Cold calling Uninvited call by a salesman with the intention of securing an interview leading to the placing of an order.

Cold canvassing Calling on prospects without warning and assessing their needs without any prearrangement.

Colour separation Photographic process whereby the colours in an illustration are filtered to produce a set of three or four negatives from which printing plates are made. *See* Four-colour set for the application involved here.

Column inches Measurement of area derived from the width of a column of type in a publication, multiplied by its depth. Column centimetres now applies under metrication and is replacing column inches in practice.

Combination Printing block which combines both line and screen (half-tone) etching.

Commando or pioneer selling Intensive selling into new markets, often with an entirely new product and sometimes by a specially employed sales force instead of or augmenting existing personnel.

Commercial Advertisement in television (or radio) either in colour or monochrome.

Commission (1) Agreed financial share of a transaction accruing to a salesman or selling agent responsible for initiating or introducing business. (2) To hire or brief another concern to undertake a defined assignment. (3) Term used to describe discount allowed to an advertising agency by media owners in consideration of its space/time purchases on behalf of clients.

Commitment (in advertising) Action whereby advertising space or time becomes chargeable at the full fee, whether cancelled or fulfilled. This occurs automatically to all bookings at a given time prior to scheduled appearance.

Common carrier Carrier prepared to transport goods of any description for anyone willing to hire its services. While it may normally specify the type or size of goods, or even the area in which it is prepared to work, providing it implies it will work for anyone it is considered to be a common carrier, whereupon it is legally obliged to carry goods when requested to do so, subject to any limitations previously publicized.

Common market Commonly used to refer to the European Economic Community, emphasizing its trading significance, but may apply in general terms to any other regional trading grouping.

Comparative analysis Comparison of quantitative factors relevant to different advertising media or vehicles, based usually on cost factors taking into account the demographic penetration of different publications.

Compensation (in advertising) Money negotiated as a refund by the agency, media or production departments for advertising which has appeared incorrectly, the fault lying, at least in part, with the publisher or contractor.

Compensation (as applied to remuneration) Amalgam of different forms of remuneration for sales executives.

Competition Existence of rival products or services within the same market (direct competition).

Competitions Promotional device, whereby prospects are invited to compete for prizes by submitting solutions to problems along with a required number of 'evidences of purchase'. Nearly always involve tie-breakers in the form of apt descriptions or advertising slogans in order to limit number of applicants for prizes, though some competitions offer a multitude of small prizes. Strictly controlled by gaming legislation.

Competitive bidding Estimating the probability of being awarded a contract based on different price levels and submitting the price that best suits the company according to its current needs.

Competitive strategy Determination of business objectives and policies through marketing intelligence, including pricing strategy.

Complementary demand Demand for one product bringing joint demand for an associated product.

Complete refund offer Offer by manufacturer to refund entire cost of purchase after a complaint by a customer. Frequently includes reimbursement of postal expenses in addition.

Composite demand Total demand for a material usable for a number of different purposes.

Concept testing Means by which a new product idea is tested for its acceptability in the market before a prototype is made. Used as a first stage in screening a new product concept. The potential benefits are put to prospective buyers and users to test their reactions to an idea. May also be used for pretesting advertisements.

Concessionaire One who operates a business or trade within premises supplied by another.

Condensed Type-face which is especially narrow thus enabling a larger number of letters per inch to be used.

Conditional sale agreement Agreement for the sale of goods, wherein the purchase price may be payable in parts and where the property in the goods remains in the hands of the seller until the terms of the agreement are fulfilled.

Confidence level   *See* Normal distribution.

Conglomerate   Holding company, generally consisting of a group of subsidiary companies engaged in dissimilar business activities, but centrally controlled.

Consideration   In a contract, the promise of one party must be supported by the agreement of the other party to do, or not to do, some act or to pay some money. The agreement by the other party is known as the consideration. If consideration does not pass, then no contract is enforceable. However, consideration, to be effective, must have some value, i.e. it must be subject to some definition in monetary terms.

Consignee   Person to whom goods are to be delivered.

Consignment note   Shipping term for a document accompanying a consignment of goods often used as an alternative to a bill of lading.

Consignment selling   Goods sent to distributors who take possession but title remains with manufacturer until consignment is paid for. *See* Sale or Return.

Conspicuous consumption   Consumption for appro-bation instead of utility; tends to be inherent in all purchases, irrespective of the actual utility of the product. Attributed to the American economist, Thorstein Veblen.

Consular invoice   Importing countries often insist that goods destined for their country are accompanied by a supporting invoice checked and stamped by their own consul in the exporting country. This enables the importing government to exercise some control over the flow of imported goods.

Consumer   Strictly, the ultimate consumer of a product, the ultimate user of a product or service; the person who derives the satisfaction or the benefit offered. The

37

'consumer' is not necessarily the customer, since there are often 'customers' in the buying/distribution chain; moreover, the consumer is frequently not the person who makes the buying decision; for instance, in the case of many household products, where the housewife may make the purchase but consumption or use is by the whole family. 'Consumer' is not normally applied to the purchase of industrial goods and services where the customer is usually a corporate body. Nevertheless, consumable goods are sold to industry for corporate purposes and the consumers of these goods can be identified for marketing practice.

Consumer advertising Loosely relating to all advertising of goods or services to the mass markets of individuals or families. Used in contrast to industrial or capital goods advertising.

Consumer affairs, Department of Known as the Fair Trading Department, this organization was set up in 1972 in the wake of growing consumerism. It is attached to the DTI, has its own Ministers of State and has staff seconded from the Consumers Association and major companies. It is headed by a Director of Fair Trading with power to recommend the imposition of regulations under the Fair Trading Act to stop loopholes where the intention of this legislation is being legally thwarted.

Consumers Association Independent non-profit-making organization established in 1950 to help shoppers by testing goods and services on sale to the public. The Association buys goods, simulating the consumer buying process anonymously and then tests them. Its findings are published in a monthly magazine, 'Which'.

Consumer behaviour Buying habits or patterns of behaviour of consuming public either in general or in specific groups.

Consumer buying power Available discretionary income; surplus after commitments have been met, but including those amounts currently committed via discretionary agreements such as hire-purchase, credit sale, or bank loan repayments which will eventually become available for future expenditure. Excludes taxation, rates and any other obligatory call upon income the consumer has no power to evade.

Consumer Council   Council of twelve people set up by the Government in 1963, following publication of the Maloney Report, and aided by the DTI (then the Board of Trade) to provide greater protection for consumers. It was disbanded in 1971 and has been replaced by the Department for Fair Trading, working under the Department of Consumer Affairs.

Consumer credit   Loans to customers to enable them to buy the seller's output. Often the seller is helped to provide credit by the resources of a finance house or other intermediary, such as Barclaycard or Access.

Consumer durables   Goods which are intended for mass markets, but are not in fact consumed immediately, but have a lasting life, e.g. washing machines, cars, furniture.

Consumerism   Movement by individuals and pressure groups designed to ensure that 'consumers' interests are safeguarded. In a society where marketing orientation is universal, consumerism would be said to be obsolescent since, by definition, the consumers' interests would be fully catered for by the competing firms. In fact, consumerism has aims which may be identified with those of marketing.

Consumer need   Reference to any desire or requirement a person (consumer) might have, whether existing and perceptible, or latent and unrecognized. The determination and evaluation of consumer needs could be said to be at the root of the marketing concept from which all subsequent activities develop. Not to be confused with consumer want.

Consumer panels Groups of consumers selected as representative of the population reporting on their purchases and purchasing behaviour. *See* Continuous research.

Consumer preferences Collective scales devised to indicate relative levels of preference for available goods and services.

Consumer satisfaction Satisfaction of a consumer want is an essential part of the marketing operation. Fundamentally, a person buys (acquires) a product or service for the satisfaction it will provide. This may be tangible or intangible (as indeed will be the 'want') but providing a product gives consumer satisfaction, a main aim of the marketing concept has been fulfilled.

Consumer surplus Difference between the actual price of a product and its maximum worth to the consumer.

Consumer want Human physiological and psychological requirements which may or may not be at a personal level of awareness. These are capable of generating psychic impulses which the 'consumer' recognizes as needs. To 'want' a product is to form a conscious desire to acquire it and is clearly different to that condition of simply experiencing a 'need' for it. The transition from 'need' to 'want' can be part of changing social behaviour as, for example, the wider use of bathrooms or it can be aided by some form of persuasion, as has been the case with deodorants. Marketing action is highly significant in this process.

Consumption Rate at which a product or commodity is consumed or used.

Container A generic term used to describe any form of pack or receptacle containing goods, liquid or solid. More often applied to large units.

Continuous billing Preparation of invoicing procedure

throughout a business period rather than at a single time each month.

Continuous research Research studies undertaken on a regular ongoing basis. Used by many sponsoring companies as a performance monitoring method.

Contract Legally binding document or situation in which a seller undertakes to supply goods or services to a buyer in 'consideration' of some financial or other return.

Contribution analysis Estimating the difference between product selling prices and their variable costs per unit, so calculating the extent to which each unit contributes to fixed costs and profits.

Controlled circulation In which the method of circulation of a publication is controlled by some specific criterion relating to the status of the reader, and for which no separate charge is made.

Convenience goods (1) Goods which are very widely distributed and which are bought more according to convenience of acquisition than by 'brand' or particular value, e.g. petrol, cigarettes. (2) Goods having an element of processing, historically carried out by customer or user, that gives an added value to the product and for which a premium price may be obtained.

Conversion value Cost of converting or assembling product plus profit. Sometimes known as 'added value'.

Conversion rate Measure of conversion of inquiries or replies to an advertisement or mailing shot into sales. *See* Response rate.

Co-operative Voluntary organization set up by producers and/or consumers to service their own needs by democratic control, distributing profit according to purchases, sales or fixed return on capital. *See* Retailers' co-operatives.

Co-operative advertising (1) Promotion by group of

concerns in the same industry. (2) Local advertising by a retail outlet in conjunction with the suppliers of a nationally advertised product.

Copy   Text or written matter for reproduction.

Copy date   Date by which advertising or editorial matter should reach a publisher for inclusion in a particular issue. *See* Press date.

Copy plan   Statement of theme(s) and other material for the development of a copy platform.

Copy platform   Main copy theme of an advertisement.

Copyright   Sole legal right to produce, or to reproduce, a work or any substantial part thereof, in any material form whatsoever.

Copy-rotation   Using a systematic rota of different advertisements in order to enhance attention and impact.

Copy test   Test of advertising copy, either before or after publication, aiming to discover readers' comprehension, interest, brand preference, company image, etc.

Copywriter   Person who writes copy for advertisements or other promotional material. Usually employed by an advertising agency, but, in technical areas, will more frequently be employed by the firm manufacturing and/or distributing the products concerned.

Cornering the market   Person or organization contriving to take advantage of a monopoly situation, during which prices and terms can be unilaterally controlled.

Corporate or prestige advertising   Any form of advertising which has as its objective the building up of a company's reputation. Has a closer affinity to public relations activity than to advertising or sales promotional activity. *See* Institutional advertising.

Corporate image   Image or impression created in the

public mind by the name or symbol of a company or organization. Also referred to as Corporate identity and having much to do with the reputation of the concern.

Corporate planning Setting down of long-term plan of development in a methodical manner, based upon all the available facts, in relating to the ultimate goals of a company and the ways it intends to achieve them. Time scales vary from three to ten years (even more in certain industries). Fundamental to the preparation of a corporate plan is the need to define exactly the area of business in which to be operative. A second requirement is that any such plan be flexible, subject to regular updating as events move to change the criteria upon which it is based.

Correlation Measure of the degree of relationship found to exist between two distinct sets of data, e.g. telephone ownership with age.

Cosmetic Refers to the appearance of a medium, particularly publications: hence the use of such expressions as, 'giving it a facelift'.

Cost and freight (C and F) Term used in foreign trade contracts, where the exporter agrees to pay the freight charges in addition to the consignment costs of getting the goods 'free on board'.

Cost benefit analysis Investigation into the social costs and social benefits of community investment projects.

Cost centre Application of responsibility accounting; a unit or centre of activity to which costs are assigned or allocated. *See* Profit centre.

Cost comparison Studying the relative costs of two or more alternatives.

Cost effectiveness Measure of most economic activity in achievement of given objective.

Cost insurance and freight (CIF) Term used in foreign trade contracts, indicating a price which includes the freight and insurance charges in addition to the charges incurred to transport the goods 'free on board'.

Cost insurance freight and interest   Term used in foreign trade contracts, where the exporter agrees to pay the freight, insurance, and interest (interest charges on the value of the goods) in addition to the charges incurred prior to 'free on board' status.

Cost of living index   Index number representing the trend of a series of prices paid by consumers for a representative sample of items, so revealing the changes in the cost to households of typical purchase needs. Known officially as the Retail Price Index.

Cost per inquiry   Cost of producing a single inquiry in an advertising campaign. Most usually expressed in the form of an average, i.e. not any particular or selected inquiry but a resultant reflecting the average cost of all inquiries received.

Cost plus   Pricing method whereby actual production costs, or an estimate thereof, is added to a profit figure to arrive at a selling price. Originally used for war contracts, the system is still used in development work where eventual costs cannot be realistically estimated. The principle is used widely in industry but as a pricing policy where historical costs, together with agreed profit margin, give the selling price.

Coupon price reductions   Making a price concession by providing coupons, of fixed value, sometimes printed upon the pack to encourage the initial and subsequent purchases. The coupon may, however, appear in a printed advertisement or be distributed direct to householders and may, or may not, require a previous purchase.

Coverage (in advertising)   Proportion (expressed in percentage terms) of a market exposed to advertising.

CPT (Cost per thousand)   Cost of reaching a thousand

potential buyers, usually of a specified demographic group, with a given advertising vehicle.

Crate Type of container, constructed of wood, often built around the product. Specially in relation to bulky heavy goods. *See* Case.

Creative Relating in advertising to the conceptual input upon which a campaign or an advertisement is based and incorporating the copy and visual content – the creative expression.

Creative department Part of an advertising agency concerned with creating ideas and expressing them in copy and design.

Creative salesmen Users of original material or ideas and their presentation in developing a sales territory.

Credibility gap Difference between commonly accepted levels of performance and the expectations aroused by extravagant claims on behalf of a person, organization, product or service.

Credit (1) Supplying goods in advance of full payment. (2) Bank credit: loans and overdrafts to bank clients. *See* Consumer credit.

Credit account (1) Purchase made on credit and account settled, monthly or otherwise by agreement. (2) Regular monthly payments made by bankers' order to retail establishment against which persons may make purchases up to an agreed multiple of the monthly instalment. (The amount is subject to Government fiscal controls over the circulation and velocity of cash within the economy and will therefore vary according to the level of economic activity.)

Credit cards Identification Cards, possession of which enables the consumer to make a range of purchases from member retailers and then settle the full amount monthly, or, alternatively over a longer period together with interest charges. Mainly but not exclusively issued by the banks in UK. Agency cards are issued chiefly for regular industrial purchases, e.g. petroleum.

Credit note   Document conveying credit of a stated amount, often against returns or allowances but most frequently adjusting errors or omissions related to previous charges.

Creditor   Party to a credit transaction who is owed money by another party involved in it.

Credit rating   Systematic rating of customers for credit worthiness.

Credit sale   Sale made on credit over a short term, where the ownership of the goods passes with possession. In the case of hire-purchase extending over a longer period, the creditor retains ownership, until a statutorily fixed portion of the debt has been paid. After this point the goods cannot legally be repossessed, although the buyer remains legally liable for the outstanding portion within the statutory period.

Credit squeeze   Government intervention over credit facilities in order to limit the rate of consumption for fiscal purposes.

Crop   To cut down in size a photograph or illustration, either to focus interest upon particular features or to make most effective use of limited space available.

Cross-elasticity of demand   Response of demand for one commodity to a change in the price of another, e.g. a transfer occurring as when the price of electricity increases, demand for less expensive alternatives, possibly gas or oil, increases.

Cumulative audience   Aggregate of persons or homes reached by successive issues or broadcasts: synonym for Cumulative reach. *See* Reach.

Currency of a bill   Period of time between the drawing of a bill of exchange and the final date when it becomes payable.

Custom-built   Made to specific individual customer specification.

Customer   Person or organization actually making the purchasing decision not necessarily the 'consumer' or 'user'. Legally, a party to a contract for the sale of goods.

Customer orientation   Preoccupation with customer needs within an effort to build a sound enterprise with prospects of growth. Basis for marketing theory and practice which dictates that competitive survival, growth and returns on investment are proper rewards for the achievement of consumer satisfaction.

Customer records   Tabulation of inquiries and orders received, deliveries, and any other pertinent information concerning a customer and his satisfaction.

Customs bills of entry   Lists published daily by the Customs and Excise authorities of ships from British ports, showing details of cargo and destinations.

Customs tariff   List of dutiable goods published by Her Majesty's Stationery Office for showing the levels of duty payable.

Cybernetics   Study of communications systems whether of human or mechanical form. Also refers to means of controlling activities in order to keep them directed at a particular objective.

Cycles of trade   Repetitive periodic movements in trade, especially in relation to upturns and recessions. Cyclical analysis of industries, for example, has been found useful in sales forecasting.

D

Daily report of calls   List of interviews obtained and visits made by salesmen, sometimes submitted daily but may be given in form of weekly summary to regional or head office.

Data   Statistical term describing classified factual information. Singular is datum.

Data processing   Arrangement of data into a systematic form and its further analysis, most frequently by mechanical or automatic means.

Data sheet   Leaflet containing factual information and data about a product and its performance.

Date coding   Practice of showing manufacturing date or, more commonly, date by which product should be sold to reach consumer in an acceptably fresh condition.

Date in charge   Date from which the rental for a poster site is charged.

Days of grace   Additional time allowed by customs for payment of a bill of exchange after the due date. Normally maximum of three days is allowed in this way.

Dead freight   Payable where the charterer is unable entirely to fill a ship with cargo and is therefore charged against empty space.

Deadline   Time by which a particular stage of a job must be completed, particularly in journalism where the story becomes dead if not completed in time. Also with advertising and broadcasting and indeed has been generally adopted as a term in planning procedure.

Dealer aid   Any material supplied to a dealer (retailer) in order to assist him in his task of selling merchandise, e.g. point-of-sale display items, leaflets, samples and dispensers.

Dealer leaders   Promotional device providing incentives to retailers to stock a product, or range of products, at predetermined quantities.

Dear money   Applies when interest rates (the price of money) are high and loans have generally become more difficult to obtain.

Debug   Logically to trace and eliminate errors from a programme (BS3527).

Decision–making unit   Group of people who together contribute to a decision on whether or not, and what to purchase (DMU). Used more in industrial marketing but can apply for example, to a consumer situation, e.g. the multiple household.

Decision tree   Display of events, past, present and future, leading to and effecting the outcome of a business decision.

Deck cargo   Cargo stowed on deck rather than in the ship's hold. Deck cargo may often be of a hazardous nature and must, therefore, be easier to jettison in a situation of jeopardy.

Deferred rebate   Rebate or discount on goods accumulated for an agreed period; used as an incentive to customers to remain loyal to supplier or to buy all needs from one supplier. A form of contract where the discount allowed is conditional upon both the total and period of the purchases.

Definition   In communications, this refers to the clarity or fidelity with which an illustration or image is reproduced.

Deflation   Reduction in the amount of available money causing incomes to fall and unemployment to grow.

Del credere agent   Agent who accepts responsibility for the payment of money due to the principal, and who earns an increased commission for taking the additional risks involved.

Delivery note Document accompanying goods on delivery to buyer. Used as a means of checking delivery, dealing with claims for shortage, damage and empties and subsequently clearing the invoice for the goods.

Demand Derived from economics, its usual reference in marketing is to the aggregate of effective purchasing intentions in a community regarding a particular product or service.

Demand function Relationship between demand and the determinants of demand such as price, substitute products, income, or credit facilities.

Demand pull Resultant of demand stimulants applied in marketing: works in conjunction, for example, with sales push.

Demand theory Branch of economic theory devoted to the analysis of demand determinants and consumers/users scales of preferences.

Demography Science of social statistics, particularly population statistics, essential to market research and effective campaign planning.

Demonstration Showing the product or service in action. Sometimes used to refer to an artificial situation where audiovisual equipment is used instead of the actual product/service itself.

Department store Large store selling a wide range of commodities, particularly clothing, where merchandise is segregated into different departments, each having a specialist manager, usually wholly responsible for own buying and selling but subject to central control. Frequently offers credit and delivery facilities to customers and usually will be located only in urban marketing centres.

Depression Period during which a nation's productive resources are persistently underemployed; often manifests itself through a long period of high unemployment among a community's labour force.

Depth interview Informal conversation between interviewer and respondent but with underlying crossexamination following clearcut objectives. Intended to discover facts which might not emerge from direct questioning.

Derived demand Indirect demand for capital goods, materials or other factors of production which are used to provide goods for which there is direct demand.

Design In marketing, used as a generic term embracing all types of visual work, e.g. roughs, typography, graphics, finished art, for all kinds of application – advertising, exhibitions, print work, house styling.

Design factor Measurement of relative efficiency of sample design against a reading of 1–0 for a completely random sample.

Desire Expression of human appetite for given object of attention.

Desk research Study of mainly external published data and material but including other already available internal information, e.g. company records.

Devaluation Reduction in the value or price of one currency or commodity relative to other currencies or commodities.

Deviation, standard Statistical term used to describe, by formula, movement of the spread of data around an average.

Diadic Paired comparison test involving informants reporting on two products or advertisements, one against the other.

Differential sampling Weighted samples adjusted to allow for known bias in penetration or spending power.

Dimension Measurable quantity, used in marketing

research to compare responses at different levels or in regard to platforms.

Diminishing returns, law of   States that where one 'factor of production' is increased while others remain constant, output will increase by steadily decreasing amounts.

Direct expenses   All costs directly attributable to a product, a project, or an accounting centre.

Direct mail   Mailing of a piece of informative literature, or of any other promotional material, to selected prospects.

Direct mail shot   One single batch or mailing in a direct mail campaign. One mailing shot might therefore comprise a large number of items and a campaign might consist of several mailing shots.

Directory   Published source of reference, usually on annual basis but possibly more frequent, setting out comprehensive coverage of companies and services in a particular area of business and/or their range of products, e.g. *Advertisers' Annual* and *BRAD*.

Direct response marketing   Selling by means of press advertisements which invite a direct placement of orders without further negotiation or intermediate channels of distribution. *See* Mail order.

Direct selling   Selling without the use of a retail outlet, distributor, broker or wholesaler or any other form of middleman.

Direct taxation   Taxes on individuals or organizations levied directly by income or wealth.

Discount   Reduction on the quoted or list price of a product, usually in the form of a percentage. Examples include discounts for prompt payment, large quantities, bulk deliveries, special sizes and deliveries at off-peak times.

Discount house   Large store or branch of chain, offering mainly durable consumables at heavily discounted prices but providing little or no handling, delivery or credit services to customers.

Discount rate   Rate at which bills of exchange are discounted. Linked with the now discontinued Bank Rate – since termed Minimum Lending Rate.

Discrimination test   Investigation aimed at discovering the incidence of customer differentiation for a product or package.

Disinflation   Fiscal control in which excess purchasing power is being syphoned off by the government in taxation.

Disparaging copy   *See* Knocking copy.

Display   Commonly used in retailing to refer to an exhibition of merchandise, whether in store or in window. Also describes panels – display boards. *See* Window dressing. May also refer to arrangement of control dials, meters and switches for industrial products.

Display advertising   Advertising other than simple typeset lineage advertisements of the classified kind. Also implies an element of design, e.g. use of display type faces as opposed to uniform body matter.

Display outer   Outer container for protecting goods in transit, which converts into a display unit at the point of sale. Usually a carton containing a convenient small quantity for counter show and dispensing.

Display pack   Pack which, in addition to performing a 'packaging' function, also serves as a means of displaying the product at the point of sale. Usually applies to single items as opposed to the display outer.

Disposable income   Residue of personal income after statutory deductions at source.

Distribution check   Survey taken at retail outlets to measure levels of distribution being achieved.

Distribution, theory of   Economic theory explaining

the determinants of the prices of 'factors of production' and their income, together with all processes and media for the distribution of goods and services available for consumption.

Distributor Firm which buys and sells on its own account but which deals in the goods of certain specified manufacturers. Common in trades where special representation, stocking and service facilities are required, e.g. motor transport.

Diversification Introduction of new products into existing markets or of existing products into new markets to extend life cycles and offset decline. Rarely involves introducing new products into new markets. Also to hedge against a company's future being tied too closely to a small number of products/outlets. Achieved either by new investment or acquisition.

Dock dues Toll on all vessels entering or leaving a dock.

Door-to-door Practice of selling by calls upon householders, may also be used to distribute promotional material. *See* Canvass.

Dormant accounts Accounts once active as customers but not now buying, for whatever reason.

Double crown Basic unit of size in posters, a sheet, size 20 ins wide by 30 ins deep.

Double-decker Two outdoor advertising panels sited one above the other.

Double front Twin poster sites arranged to utilize both sides of the front of a bus or other commercial vehicle. Usually each a 'single sheet' or smaller.

Double page spread Two facing pages in a magazine or newspaper, used in advertising as if they were one single sheet, i.e. the design carries right across the gutter in the centre.

Down time Period during which a machine is not

operative due to mechanical failure, machine adjustment, nonavailability of materials, labour or maintenance work. Average down-time is built into product prices to ensure that such hidden costs are covered by sales revenue.

Drawback Rebate on duty paid for imported goods when used in the manufacture of products for export.

Drawing accounts Credit made available to salesmen in anticipation of future earnings most usually operative where a substantial part of remuneration derives from a commission on sales. Particularly related to industrial goods, for example, where the number of sales over time is low but the value of each is comparatively high.

Drop shipment Describes arrangement where goods are not shipped by person or organization receiving the initial order; commonly a despatch by wholesaler, retailer or agent on advice from manufacturing or marketing company.

Drum Large cylindrical metal container mainly used for bulk packaging of liquids. Term can also apply to a small fibreboard cylinder often with metal end closures and containing powders in convenient quantities for household use, e.g. salt, custard powder and abrasive cleaning products.

Dry-run Pretransmission television rehearsal where action, lines, cues, etc. are perfected.

Dubbing Superimposing sound upon an already completed film, as opposed to simultaneous recording.

Dummy Simplified representation of a proposed publication, package, or other promotional item. *See* Mockup.

Dump display Unit of fibreboard or woven wire into which a quantity of products is exposed in random order for self-selection at a retail outlet. Particularly associated with supermarkets in connection with product launches or clearances and carrying special price or other offers.

Dumping Distribution of goods overseas at a price much less than the equivalent in market of origin and which would not normally be expected to make a full contribution to the recovery of overheads.

Duplication (in advertising) Extent to which the audience of one medium or vehicle overlaps that of another.

Dustbin check Survey at consumer level to establish level of purchases over an agreed period according to brand and pack. Emptied containers are retained in a bin known as a dustbin. It is a form of household audit for which greater reliability is claimed because tangible evidence of consumption is provided.

Dutch auction Bidding starting at a high price and reducing until a bid is made. Most often associated with charities but may be used as a method of sales promotion which gains an audience for a required exposure or demonstration.

Duty free shop Retail establishment in which selling prices do not include Customs and Excise duties and may, therefore, be fixed at a lower level than those prevailing generally within a particular country. Most often located at air or seaports where operators can, as a result take a higher margin of profit than other retailers.

E

Ear Advertising space at top left or right of a newspaper's front page.

Econometrics Application of mathematical/statistical techniques to the solution of economic problems, usually with the aid of electronic data processing devices.

Economic Community (European) *See* Common Market.

Economic dynamics Analysis of economic systems, through time, and particularly in relation to behaviour of markets, firms and the national economy in general.

Economic growth Increase in productive capacity for entire economy with the result of increasing national income.

Economic price Price which includes full consideration of elements of direct and indirect costs together with an allowance for the opportunity cost.

Economic rent Earning differential between the most efficient and alternative uses of a factor of production.

Economies of scale Reduction in unit cost attributable to overheads being divided over a larger volume, often due to introduction of mechanization or automation leading to greater output at lower overall cost.

Editorial advertisement Advertisement designed in the form of a piece of editorial matter. Such advertisements must, however, be clearly labelled 'advertisement'.

Editorial matter News or entertainment section of publication or broadcast, i.e. excluding any advertising matter it may carry.

Editorial publicity Space in a journal or newspaper in which a product, service, or company is discussed or publicized at the discretion of the editor. *See* Press relations.

Ego Term borrowed from psychology, indicating an individual's conception of himself, often having an influence over his purchasing behaviour patterns.

Elasticity Measure of the degree of responsiveness of one variable (the dependent variable) to changes in another (the independent variable), where a causal relationship is observed to exist.

Electrotype Duplicate of an original printing block; produced by electrochemical deposition onto a matrix. Commonly known as 'electro'.

Embargo (1) Restriction on the import of certain specified goods into a country. The embargo may be imposed either by the importing country or the exporting country. (2) In relation to news releases, a time or date before which a particular item of news must not be published.

Emotions Arguably defined as bodily changes, together with mental change, influencing one's decisions, sometimes out of the normal pattern for the individual, used particularly in reference to buying behaviour.

Empathy Identifying oneself completely with the problems and aspirations of others; often used in connection with the necessity for a salesman to see his task through his customers' eyes and to establish a reciprocity with them effective in concluding business agreements.

ENAB Evening Newspaper Advertising Bureau. Sales organization designed to promote the use of local evening newspapers by national advertisers.

Endorsement Transfer of the property in a bill of exchange by the signature of the owner. Increasingly used to indicate some amendment to the original composition of a contract or legal document.

Enquiry In business terms, 'inquiry is preferred to enquiry' to distinguish between a general request for information (enquiry) and a firm request for details prior to placing an order (inquiry). *See* Inquiry.

Entrepot trade Business consisting of re-exporting of imported goods, with or without any additional processing.

Environment Refers to surrounding conditions of an activity, particularly in marketing, the social, physical and psychological conditions.

Equilibrium price Price at which supply equals demand and there is no tendency to change, upwards or downwards.

Ergonomics Study concerned with the working environment and its effect on a person's efficiency with a view to applying anatomical, physiological and psychological knowledge to the solution of problems which may arise from this relationship.

Estimating Strictly, producing an estimate of the cost/price of an activity particularly in one-off jobs and in contracting. Term sometimes applied to the calculation of a price upon which a firm quotation is based. Almost entirely confined to industrial goods and services but also used in the case of some consumer durables.

Ethical advertising Advertising of ethical phar-maceutical products addressed to the medical profession. Also applied generally to describe honest, informative advertising, as distinct from unscrupulous and misleading practice. *See* Codes of practice. *See also* Voluntary controls.

Eurodollar American currency (dollars) held either by individuals or organizations outside the United States.

European Economic Community Signatories to the Treaty of Rome for the creation of a customs union or common market. *See* Common Market. *See also* Economic Community (European).

European Free Trade Association Association of certain European countries, not members of the European Economic Community, set up in 1959 to develop free trade between members.

Ex ante Ex ante demand is the level of demand for commodities which are expected to be bought at a certain given price.

Excess capacity Existence of more productive capacity

than is warranted by the demand existing at any given time.

Excess demand Existence of more demand than presently existing productive capacity is able to satisfy.

Exchange rate Fixed price at which one currency may be exchanged for another or for gold. A floating exchange rate exists when the rate is not fixed but is allowed to find its own level in trading negotiations.

Excise duty Tax on the production of particular goods in high general demand, such as alcoholic drinks, tobacco and petroleum goods.

Exclusive In press relations, relates to a story and/or illustratory photographic or other material which is supplied to one publication alone.

Exclusive agency agreement Agreement binding two parties, one as principal, the other as agent, involving a product, a market, or a geographical area, being limited in availability to the agent for a period, and fully supported by the principal.

Ex gratia As a matter of favour. Usually refers to payments which are made where no legal obligation exists to make them.

Exhibition Putting on display a company's products or services for promotional purposes. Particularly the gathering of a number of such displays which are either on view to the public in general or merely to invited guests. May be commercially or privately sponsored.

Expanded type Typeface in printing which has wider dimensions than is usual. Its use is intended to exert a greater dominance or legibility.

Exponential smoothing Statistical process applied to moving averages, to reflect most recent changes in a series of data.

Export Credits Guarantee Department Usually abbreviated to ECGD. UK government facility for exporters established in 1930 as an independent department with authority under ministerial policy control to issue insurance policies against loss incurred through insolvency, default, nonacceptance of delivery or political measures outside the control of the insuring company.

Export declaration   Details, to be submitted within six days, of the export of all goods from the country.

Export house   Organization specializing in selling into foreign markets. Originally called Forwarding agents, they now provide a large range of services to exporters big or small. Representative body is the Institute of Freight Forwarders.

Export, Institute of   Institution set up in 1926 to foster conditions in which exporting can be profitably expanded in the interests of the UK community as a whole.

Ex post   Actual value attributable to a variable factor. Ex post demand, for example, is the actual quantity bought at the price realizable.

Extended use tests   Similar to placement tests but used, especially in industrial marketing, where it is necessary for findings to be derived from use of the product in a work situation over a long term period.

Extensive selling   Selling products through every conceivable distribution channel, stocking in every possible retail outlet, and promoting sales to every likely market segment.

Extrapolation   *See* Projection.

Ex works price   Basic price of a product at the point of manufacture, i.e. excluding delivery and insurance, and sometimes packaging.

Eye movement camera   Used in advertising research, this equipment tracks the movement of the eye over press advertisements, showing the path which the eye takes and indicating the sequence of interest that the features arouse.

Eye observation camera Equipment used in advertising research to measure pupil dilation, so giving indications of arousal of informant.

F

Face In printing, a particular design or style of lettering upon which a typeface is based. Two broad categories, 'serif' and 'sans serif' distinguish between the more and less intricate characters.

Face value Nominal value or price of a commodity.

Facia In exhibitions, the headboard above a stand. Sometimes used for advertising purposes, e.g. featuring a brand-name, but usually carries the identity of the exhibitor.

Facing matter Positioning of an advertisement so that it appears opposite an editorial page.

Factor analysis Study of the component parts of an attitude research programme interview with the aim of discovering more meaningful conclusions than are apparent from the data taken as a whole.

Factoring (1) Discounting of bills. (2) Middlemen acting as go-between for sellers of commodities without a common interest. The factor arranges for the sale of products of both companies and then settles the accounts. Factors are often involved in processing as well as the usual wholesaling operations. Otherwise, they would be purely marketing agencies.

Feature In press relations, an article or story which is written in some depth and at some length; usually exclusive.

Feed (1) To supply information to another, particularly on sales leads. (2) Relaying transmission of a broadcast from one station to another.

Feedback   Response or reaction to a message, indicating to its communicator how the message is being interpreted.

Fibreboard   Two or more sheets of paperboard pasted together to form a stronger, thicker material. Usually a combination of kraft and chipboard. Solid fibreboard is a straightforward laminate often used, for example, as a book cover. Corrugated fibreboard comprises two outer 'liners' in between which is sandwiched a corrugated 'fluting'. Both types of fibreboard are used extensively in the construction of 'cases', sometimes referred to as containers or cartons.

Fibreboard case   Container constructed from either solid or corrugated fibreboard, intended for protection of goods during transit. A transit outer.

Field force   Team of interviewers used for gathering information direct from respondents in or around the respondents' usual habitat. To be carefully distinguished from sales force.

Field organization   Structure governing the operation of a field force, which may be for purposes of marketing research or act as a promotional device.

Fieldwork   That part of a market research survey which involves face-to-face interviews with respondents by research investigators, as compared with other means of obtaining data, such as postal or telephone enquiries and the searching of relevant published material. *See* Desk research.

Film rush   First print of ciné film sequence; produced immediately after shooting in order to see whether a retake is necessary. *See* Rush.

Film strip   Joined sequence of positive transparencies either black and white but more usually in colour. Each strip consists of a limited number of exposures, which together tell a story or put across a message. Often produced in conjunction with a sound script which can either be spoken during showing or coupled electronically for automatic reproduction.

Filter (1) Means of eliminating unnecessary information. (2) Receptionist or secretary protecting executive(s) from unexpected callers. (3) Question in research questionnaire intended to redirect interview.

Final Proof or pull of the corrected, locked-up printing forme or of a block, showing the printed corrected work as it will eventually appear. It is thus distinguished from initial proofing which is for checking and correcting purposes only.

Fine grain Descriptive of a photographic emulsion or the developer used to process it; results in a negative which can be enlarged to a high degree without showing excessive graining.

Fine screen In printing, a halftone screen containing 100 or more lines to the inch.

Firm quotation Quoted price and/or conditions which will remain unchanged, subject to previously defined criteria.

First in, first out (FIFO) Principle used in stock-holding policy.

Fiscal policy Government policy in matters of taxation, particularly in controlling changing patterns of demand to meet other needs of the economy as a whole.

Fixed costs Accounting term referring to costs that are not expected to vary up to a given level of output.

Fixed spot Television spot for which a premium is paid (normally 15%) to ensure that it is transmitted within a preselected break during a programme.

Flat rate Uniform rate for advertising space or time, i.e. without allowing for discounts.

Flip chart Large white paper fold-over pad used for

conveying sales messages and making sales presentations. Used also in conferences, seminars and training courses.

Floorwalker Store security officer, usually mixing with customers and attempting to spot shoplifters.

Foil Thin film of metal, usually aluminium, used in packaging. Often referred to as tin foil or silver paper.

Folio Numbered sheet of copy.

Font *See* Fount.

Footage Indicates the length of a piece of film. Each foot contains 16 frames; 35 mm films run at $1\frac{1}{2}$ feet or 24 frames per second.

Foreigners Private work undertaken by artisans for the customers of their employers with or without the employer's approval or knowledge.

Forme Frame with typematter and blocks assembled in it for letterpress printing.

Forty-eight sheet Very large poster. *See* Bulletin board. *See also* Double crown.

Forward delivery (1) Deliveries booked in advance to meet fixed schedules. (2) Time lag between order and delivery.

Forwarding agents Packaging and shipping specialists. *See* Export house.

Forward market Market in futures, where contracts are made to buy commodities or securities at prices then ruling but for delivery at a future date.

Foul bill of lading Covers goods known to be defective; also known colloquially as a dirty bill.

Fount Complete set of type of same face and size.

Four-colour set Set of printing blocks or plates, one for each of the four major printing colours (red, yellow, blue, black) used to produce a full colour reproduction. Term sometimes refers to a set of colour proofs. *See* Colour separation. *See also* Progressives.

C

Four sheet Poster size of growing popularity, equal to four double crown posters.

Frame One individual exposure upon a reel of film.

Franchise Trading agreement, most often between a supplier and a retail outlet, where co-operation and support, often of promotional facilities, are provided to the retail outlet by the supplier as part of a contractual arrangement in return for a guarantee of sales income. A distribution device of growing importance particularly for service industries.

Franking Printing or cancellation of postage upon envelopes or labels which can be used to carry an advertising slogan.

Free alongside ship (FAS) All charges being met by the exporter up to the point of delivering to the ship.

Freeboard Distance between main deck and the waterline.

Free gifts Promotional gifts: (1) Mail-in: inviting prospective customers to send for a gift. (2) On-pack: gift attached to product at point of sale. (3) On-pack offer: inviting purchasers to send for gift, usually with evidence of a minimum purchase.

Freelance Journalist not on the staff of one newspaper, but usually contributing to several. Also refers to artists, writers and other selfemployed suppliers of specialist services.

Free market One in which forces of supply and demand are allowed to operate unhampered by government or other regulations.

Free on board (FOB) All charges being met by exporter to the point where goods are loaded on board the transit vessel.

Freesheets Local newspapers or magazines which are distributed without charge, depending for their revenue entirely on advertising support. Most of the space in these publications is sold for advertising, leaving little room for editorial content.

Free trade International trade operating without intervention of governmental restrictions or requirements.

Freight forward Convention dictating that freight charges are payable at port of destination.

Freight liner Door-to-door container service provided by British Rail.

Frequency Number of times an advertising message is delivered within a set period of time.

Fringe accounts Low profit customers making marginal contributions to a supplier's turnover and therefore liable to least service or even closure in times of financial stringency.

Front cover First page of magazine or journal, sometimes available for advertising. *See* Back cover.

Full plate Photographic print, approximate size 8 in by 6 in; sometimes known as Whole plate.

Full-line forcing Selling a whole range of products as a result of maintaining a monopoly position for one or more of the constituent products which are essential.

Futures Refers to forward sales or forward purchases. A feature of markets used to guard against violent fluctuations in price.

G

Galley First proofs of typesetting taken prior to the make-up of pages.

Gap analysis Methodical tabulation of all known 'consumer wants' of a particular product category, together with a cross-listing of the features of existing products which satisfy those wants. Such a chart shows up any gaps which exist and thus provides a pointer as to where new products might find an unfulfilled demand.

GATT General Agreement on Tariffs and Trade. International agreement signed in 1947 by numerous countries to liberalize trade by the reduction and removal of tariff barriers and quota restrictions. The agreement has no legal force but has had considerable influence in post-war developments.

Gearing Description of capital structure in limited companies referring to proportion of capital, whether debentures, preference, or ordinary shares making up total equity in the company. High gearing refers to a greater proportion of 'loan capital', i.e. debentures or preference shares, to risk capital, i.e. ordinary shares and vice versa with 'low gearing'.

Generic term In marketing, applied to brand names which have come to be adopted as the general descriptive term for a product, often as the result of extensive promotion, e.g. Hoover, Biro, Linoleum.

Geographical concentration Limiting of a sales or promotional campaign to a particular geographical region.

Geometric mean Term used in advertising schedule building where three elements (cost effectiveness, market penetration, and advertising unit cost) are treated as being entitled to an equal share of the advertising appropriation. By using the technique, selected media are given shares of the appropriation according to the extent to which they provide combinations of the three elements.

Gestation period Length of time which elapses between an initial inquiry for a product and the placing of an order. More often applied to capital goods where it can amount to several years.

GHI Guaranteed Home Impressions. A guaranteed number of television or radio advertisement impacts for a given sum of money.

Giffen goods   Goods for which demand moves in the same direction as price, instead of following the classical laws of supply and demand.

Gimmick   Idea or object which is novel or highly unusual within the context in which it is used. Lends news value to promotional activity; also helps to establish identity for a product image.

Give-away   Inexpensive promotional piece, sometimes merely a leaflet, designed for wide distribution from offices or shops or direct to prospective customers. *See* Handbill.

Give-away magazines   Magazines depending entirely on advertising for their revenues and distributed to readers free of charge. *See* Freesheets. *See also* Controlled circulation.

Goods on approval   Goods, usually of a durable character, provided for a period of trial prior to a purchasing decision and returnable in the absence of such a decision.

Goods on consignment   An arrangement whereby an agent takes possession of goods but no title to them. The agent will normally be working for a commission on their sale and the goods are returnable in the absence of a buyer being found for them.

Goodwill   That part of the value of a business enterprise reflecting consideration of its established market connections, reputation and image. On sale, that part of the purchase price not accounted for by its total net assets.

Gravure   *See* Photogravure.

Gresham's law   States that bad money drives out good, i.e. where two coins with identical face value have a different bullion content, the more valuable coin will be taken out of circulation. A similar situation may often happen in marketing where inferior goods can create a poor market reception for sound goods.

Gripe session   Refers to a conference or other meeting at which sales people primarily offer complaints about company products, personnel policy or environment. Usually taken to be a symptom of poor motivation but may also reflect lack of positive planning by the management.

Gross domestic product (GDP) Total output of goods and services by the national economy in a full year.

Gross margin Difference between cost or purchase price and the selling price for a particular piece of merchandise.

Gross reach Total number of opportunities for people to see the advertisements contained in a schedule; the sum total of the readership of each publication multiplied by the total number of insertions.

Group discussion Research technique in which a group of people is encouraged to express freely views and opinions on a selected subject. This might relate to the message contained in an advertisement, or any other component of a campaign upon which a viewpoint is sought. Group discussions are frequently used as a means of determining both overt and subconscious attitudes and motivation and discussion may range widely around the topic, a controlling psychologist ensuring that the topic is fully explored. The recorded proceedings are then subjected to further analysis. *See* Brainstorming.

Group interview Structured interview used for testing commercials or aimed at getting representative family views about a product.

Guarantee Undertaking by one party to answer for liability, or to perform a duty on the default of another, either in service or a product for which it is primarily responsible. The guarantee usually specified the extent of the liability of the guarantee. Since the Supply of Goods (Implied Terms) Act, 1973 the extent of liability is governed by statute.

Gut feeling Hunch; opinion based upon intuitive grasp

of a situation, arising from experience rather than logical deduction.

Gutter Margin of a page adjacent to the fold in a publication; the vertical centre of a double page spread.

H

Hackneyed Words or expressions which are banal or over-used: perhaps the most familar in marketing is 'new'.

Haggle Process of discussional bargaining, prior to the negotiating of prices or terms of agreement.

Halftone Printing block or plate of a tonal illustration, the reproduction of which is facilitated by breaking up the continuous tones to leave a series of dots which pick up the ink.

Halo effect (1) Describes the situation in which estimation may be coloured by the circumstances of the environment, e.g. in marketing, a company stance of frank sincerity will tend to add to a buyer's confidence in a product or service. (2) Statistical term of measurement applied to this area.

Handbill Form of printed advertising delivered personally into the hands of likely prospects. *See* Give away. *See also* Circular.

Hand held Film shot made without the use of a tripod.

Handout Inexpensive leaflet for free distribution at exhibitions or for promotional purposes, especially at point-of-sale.

Hard-boiled, Hard-headed Buyers, often with long experience, who habitually challenge or reject any new approach, organization, product or opportunity; such behaviour may be natural to the person or assumed in an effort to contain aggressive selling practices. Salesmen must be trained to anticipate and overcome sales resistance of this kind.

Headline Dominant line of type in printing or abbreviated statement in broadcasting; intended to particularize the essence of a longer, more complex message, to which attention is thus drawn.

Head-on position Outdoor advertising position directly facing traffic.

Hedging Negotiation of contractual arrangements intended to protect a buyer or seller against changes in price, supply or other conditions which may be to his disadvantage.

Her Majesty's Customs and Excise UK government department administering controls over imports and exports and the manufacture of dutiable goods together with the assessment and collection of customs duty on such goods; it is responsible internally for administering VAT (Value Added Tax) in UK.

Heuristic An adjective used to describe an exploratory method of tackling a problem, in which the solution is discovered by evaluations of the progress made towards the final result, e.g. guided trial and error. (BS 3527)

Hidden value Value not obvious at first sight. Marketing activity often constitutes such a hidden value but this should not be appreciated as such by customers unless the supplier chooses to exert effort to inform them.

High key An illustration in which the majority of tones in the subject or image lie at the light end of the grey scale.

Hire purchase An agreement for the bailment of goods under which the bailee may buy the goods or under which the property of the goods will or may pass to the bailee. Governed in UK by a series of Hire Purchase Acts, legislation which is frequently being reviewed and augmented in modern times.

Hoarding (1) Withholding money or goods from circulation for later advantage. (2) Site for poster advertising.

Holistic evaluation Evaluation of an advertising or marketing campaign as a whole, quite separately from consideration of its constituent parts.

Horizontal publication Business publication aimed at readers in similar job categories over a variety of different industries, e.g. *Management Today. See* Vertical circulation.

Hot shop Creative studio which puts high value on novelty and topicality in the preparation of its advertising copy and designs.

House agency An advertising agency wholly owned and operated by a large business organization to which it provides services which are, however, not necessarily exclusive to that organization. Similarly such an organization may additionally or alternatively use the services of independent agencies.

Household Designation of the single family unit for research survey purposes.

House magazine Periodical published by a company or other organization for public relations and/or sales promotional purposes. Usually in one of two main forms, either purely external for influencing custom, or internal for employee motivation, although the former may be circulated internally and the latter known by those outside the firm's employ. Also known as House organ.

House style Characteristic and standardized form which is applied throughout a company to such items as letter headings, publications, advertisements, vehicles and packaging. Usually includes a distinctive logotype design for instant recognition.

House-to-house Calling direct on potential consumers

and users at their own homes for purposes of distributing or collecting information, leaving samples or direct selling.

Hypermarket Larger self-service unit with minimum sales area of 2500 square metres offering an assortment of food and non-food merchandise at popular prices; often provides extensive parking facilities and associated with out-of-town shopping; often called superstores but to be distinguished from discount houses. Operation varies between retailer providing a number of shopping departments or, more usually, a site operation leasing space to different kinds of retail concerns.

I

IBA (Independent Broadcasting Authority) Statutory body consisting of a chairman, deputy chairman and eleven members who build, own and operate transmitting stations, select and appoint programme contractors, control programmes (ensuring that they comply with the provisions of the Television and Broadcasting Acts), control the advertising (ensuring that frequency, amount and nature also accord with these Acts). Since 1971, when the name was changed from Independent Television Authority, also responsible for commercial radio broadcasting. Under investigation by Annan Committee at time of going to press.

Iceberg principle Psychological concept suggesting human personality is similar in appearance to that of an iceberg, with innate desires hidden deep down under the surface. Advertisers recognize that influencing people to move in any given direction frequently demands an appeal to their less apparent desires.

ILR (Independent Local Radio) General term referring to commercial radio stations controlled by the IBA in Britain.

Image Composite mental picture formed by people

about an organization or its products, e.g. brand image, conception of a product in the market place.

Impact   Force with which an advertising or promotional message registers in a person's mind.

Impression cover   Number of insertions it takes to cover the required percentage of population actually seeing the advertisement or commercial.

Impulse purchase   One made without careful prior consideration, i.e. on the spur of the moment or even in contradiction to normal buying behaviour and sometimes without apparent rational or logical justification.

Imputed costs   Sum of opportunity costs for economic resources employed in an organization.

Incentive/reusable packs   Promotional device offering attractive containers available for some subsequent use by the consumer. Frequently encountered in food and drink products.

Income   Flow of payments accruing to individual or organization during a stated period of time. Also known as revenue and usually contrasted with expenditures in the same period for budgetary or accounting purposes.

Income distribution   National income divided among households to produce an average, useful for comparison with other markets.

Income velocity of circulation   Measurement of the rate at which money is circulating through an economy.

Independent variable   Variable subject to chance or choice factors which has an observed causal effect upon the behaviour of other variables.

Indexing   Statistical term describing a method of standardizing the base for comparative data in a time series, usually equating the initial measure to 100 and then expressing all other data in exact relation to that base; e.g.

the index of wholesale prices in any year by comparison with a base year of 100 might stand at 92 or 108 to indicate a fall or rise of 8% respectively.

Industrial advertising Advertising of products or services to industrial, commercial or business organizations. Usually relates to industrial or technical products but essentially refers to any purchase of goods or services which might be made by any such organization to distinguish it from advertising directed at consumer markets.

Industrial selling Selling to industry for industrial consumption, e.g. catering or fuel products, but more usually goods required to further production, e.g. raw materials and machinery.

Inertia selling Goods delivered to a prospect upon a sale-or-return basis without the previous consent or knowledge of the prospect. Legally, the recipient is not obliged to retain or pay for such goods and has the right of disposal in UK if reasonable notice is first given to the sender.

Inferior goods (1) Relative term denoting goods the demand for which tends to fall as incomes of their purchasers rise. (2) Descriptive term relating to goods not of a required standard.

Inflation An economic phenomenon in which decreasing purchasing power of a currency is caused by a persistent tendency of prices to rise, often sharply. Compare with deflation.

Informant Person answering or supplying answers to research questions. *See* Respondent.

Inland waterways Network of canals, rivers, and locks intended for conveyance of goods but, due to the competition of faster means of transport, is often used nowadays for pleasure craft and the provision of marinas.

Inner pack One of a number of packs which are then

stored in multiple containers, e.g. twenty individual cartons of cigarettes might be wrapped as a unit, a number of which are then packed in a fibreboard case.

Innovation Introduction of new thoughts, policies, products, markets, distribution, merchandising or other deliberate change. Given that, all things being equal, all products have a life cycle which dictates that, at some point, their usefulness will decline, innovation is an essential ingredient to long-term development of commercial enterprise and its absence must lead to the decline of the enterprise itself.

Inquiry The initial request from a prospective buyer or user for information, often following some form of advertising or sales promotion, usually with a particular purchase in mind or consideration. *See* Sales lead.

Inquiry test Method of testing advertisements or media by comparing the number of inquiries received. *See* Cost per inquiry.

Insert Piece of sales promotional material placed into the pages of a publication, either loosely or bound in. Sometimes encountered as 'inset' but this usage is not recommended since 'inset' more usually refers to the insertion of a separate photograph or chart within an overall illustration.

Insertion weights Used for weighting advertising expenditure; means of varying expenditure according to the impression value of alternative publications. It reflects the likelihood of an advertisement being seen.

Instalment selling Involves taking an initial deposit against goods purchased and collecting the balance of the selling price over an agreed period of time in fixed instalments.

Instant Term frequently applied to preprepared products of high convenience value, especially foodstuffs.

Institutional advertising *See* Corporate advertising, to which it is very similar. Institutional advertising, however, refers especially to advertising undertaken for whole industries rather than to individual corporations, e.g. Eat More Fruit.

Intaglio   Printing from a depressed surface.

Intensive interview   Technique used in marketing research to endeavour to formulate a true pattern of human behaviour by a process of continued patient probing into beliefs and desires.

Intensive selling   Selling a greater volume to present customers through energetic promotional drive.

Interface   Meeting between two or more parties whose differing interests have in some way to be reconciled.

Interfirm comparisons   Service pioneered in the UK by the British Institute of Management in which information is mutually exchanged between firms, usually in the same business, upon a confidential basis, with a view to establishing objective, practical criteria against which to evaluate comparative levels of activity and performance.

Intermedia comparisons   Comparing one medium against another or others according to cost, characteristics of the audience, and the atmosphere of the audience. *See* Intramedia comparisons.

International Monetary Fund   An institution arising from the Bretton Woods Agreement in 1944, the fund being established from 1946. Its primary object is to maintain and stabilize international rates of exchange. It is also expected to provide facilities for arranging multilateral clearing systems and to help to eliminate restrictions on international trade. The IMF is often used by countries as a world bank, particularly when facing balance of payment difficulties, each country having drawing rights against present and anticipated contributions to the fund.

Interpolation   Mathematical term referring to the technique of judging a value or values between known value points. More generally, it may be used to describe the process of drawing conclusions from known data.

Interview (1) Contact between parties, either face-to-face or through a communications medium, e.g. telephonic or postal means. (2) Market research interviewer obtaining information. (3) Salesmen giving information and obtaining data as basis for a sales transaction.

Intramedia comparisons Comparing publications or channels one against another or others within the same medium. *See* Intermedia comparisons.

Inventory (1) Complete detail of a company's assets. (2) Complete detail of values of raw materials, work in progress, and finished goods. (3) Frequently used as synonymous with stock.

Invisible exports Items such as financial services, included in the current balance of payments, that are not physically tangible as exports.

Invitation to treat Retailers putting goods on show in shop windows or display cabinets are inviting people to make an offer – the retailer is not, as is popularly believed, making any offer. Customers make the offer and, by so doing, enable the shopowner to accept. The term is a legal expression for this principle which, of course, applies equally to advertisements and to the use of illustrated catalogues as sales media.

Invoice Document listing the charges being set against a buyer in consideration of goods or services supplied. A bill.

Invoice discount Obtaining credit on the security of book debts (money owed) as a discount. Applies to companies with money tied up with debtors, especially finance houses.

Island position Advertisement surrounded entirely by editorial or margin. Also known as Solus position.

Island site Exhibition stand surrounded on all four sides by gangways.

Issue readership (average) Number of readers, on average, who read a publication.

ITCA (Independent Television Companies Association) Association of programme contractors formed to represent their mutual interests.

ITV (Independent Television) Generic term referring to the organization controlled in UK by the IBA, consisting of fourteen geographically separate television areas.

J

Jar (1) A wide mouthed container, usually of glass, stoneware, or plastic (BS 3170). (2) Glass container usually for high viscosity materials such as pastes and greases.

Jerque note Certificate issued by Customs when they are satisfied that cargo is in order.

JICNARS (Joint Industry Committee for National Readership Surveys) UK Committee comprising members representing the IPA (agencies), ISBA (advertisers), and Newspaper and Periodical Contributors Committee (NPCC). The committee issues and controls the official industry contract for national readership surveys.

JICPAS (Joint Industry Committee for Poster Audience Research) Represents IPA and ISBA in order to obtain data on poster audiences. *See* JICNARS.

JICRAR (Joint Industry Committee for Radio Audience Research) Composed of representatives of IPA, ISBA and Independent Radio Companies (ARIC); this committee operates like JICNARS to govern the issue of radio audience research figures.

JICTAR (Joint Industry Committee for Television Advertising Research) Represents IPA, ISBA and Independent Television Companies (ITCA) in a manner similar to JICNARS but is solely concerned with TV audience research.

Jingle Short tune to which the advertising message of a television, radio, or cinema commercial is sung. Not necessarily an original tune since often different words are sung to an already familiar tune.

Job evaluation Determination of the value of a job in relative or absolute terms, usually with a view to fixing the rate of pay, but also has a motivation aspect.

Job selling (1) Disposing of unwanted remainders in bulk and at a low price. (2) Selling units, usually capital equipment produced in low volume, against limited demand and established specification.

Job specification Definition of tasks to be undertaken in relation to a specific job category. Also includes responsibilities and functions in connection with other activities within an organization.

Journey planning Organizing the salesman's route, rate(s) of call, and customer priority rating so as to make his selling as cost effective as possible. *See* Call rate.

Justify To adjust the position of words on a printed page so that the left or the right hand margin is regular (BS 3527).

K

Kerbside conferences Post-interview discussion between a salesman and his sales supervisor, involving analysis of selling method, performance and achievement.

Key factors Essential elements of a given marketing or

other situation, i.e. those factors which are crucial to achieving a specified goal.

Key prospects Group of buyers within a market who hold the greatest proportionate potential purchasing power.

Keyed advertisement Advertisement designed to cause an enquirer to indicate the source of his information, for instance by including a code number or a particular 'department' within the return address.

Knocking competition Deriding the quality of competitors' products or services.

Knocking copy Advertisement copy which deliberately exposes competitive products to adverse comparison(s).

L

Laminate Two or more sheets of material bonded together either to produce simply a thicker, stronger medium, or, where different materials are laminated, to combine various desired properties. An example of the latter would be a foil-laminated board which provides a decorative finish with a rigid base.

Landscape Describes an illustration or piece of print where the width is greater than its height.

Last in first out (LIFO) Principle frequently used by trade union negotiators considering redundancy plans.

Laundromat Mechanically operated laundry using vending machines and often operating as part of a franchising operation or alternatively by a concessionaire arrangement.

Layout Accurate position guide of an advertisement or piece of literature showing the location of each visual element in relation to the other in order to permit review before printing commences. *See* Visual.

Leading In printing, putting space into text or typematter usually between lines. This is achieved by locking lead blocks into the printing forme.

Lead time Time elapsing between receipt of an order and its completion. *See* Gestation period.

Leaflet Printed piece of paper, single or folded-over to make four pages. It can be stitched with additional sheets to make into more pages. Term is, however, usually applied to a publication with no more than twelve pages, i.e. three folded sheets. *See* Brochure.

Least squares Statistical technique for identifying best fitting trend line through a collection of non-linear data points.

Legal tender Form of money which is acceptable in legal settlement of a debt. In UK, Bank of England notes of any denomination up to any amount and 'silver' up to £2.

Legend Title or description of an illustration. *See* Caption.

Legion (Advertising Data Ltd.) Independent company which analyses published advertising and provides (for a fee) media expenditure statistics relative to particular companies/organizations. *See* MEAL.

Letter of credit Document issued by a bank supporting a transaction, usually for foreign trade. A stronger guarantee is provided by the so-called 'irrevocable' letter of credit.

Letter of indemnity Document guaranteeing to cover another party against loss or default.

Letterpress Common form of commercial printing. Consists of raised printing surfaces bearing characters upon which ink is deposited and subsequently transferred to paper.

Licencing Legal arrangement transferring the rights to

manufacture, or to market, a product to another. Such an arrangement, also known as franchising, is usually formalized by contract in which there is a consideration, perhaps in the form of a regular fee, or of a commission or royalty. For the licencing company, it represents a means of expanding demand from new markets, without incurring a high speculative investment. For the licencee, it reduces the need to generate new product development, facilitates lower setting up and operating costs and thereby diminishes the degree of business risk.

Life cycle Descriptive term for the stage of life, of childhood, teenage, young marrieds with children, middle age and retirement. Mostly used in market research.

Life cycle (Product life cycle) Term relating to a generally accepted hypothesis that all products are subject to a pattern of demand which after it starts, grows, stabilizes for a period, then tends to decline and finally disappear. Whilst demand curves differ in rates of change, shape and time span, the life cycle contention is that all products have both a beginning and an end. This dictates the need for new product development; the order of time scale determines the intensity with which such development takes place.

Limited liability company Joint-stock company, being an association of persons recognized in law as a corporate personality, each enjoying limited liability as regulated by the 1862 and subsequent Companies Acts. This structure has been adopted by most well-known companies of a size greater than can be conveniently managed as a partnership.

Lineage Method of charging for classified advertising by the line.

Linear programming Any procedure for locating the maximum or minimum of a linear function of variables which are subject to linear constraints and inequalities (BS 3527).

Line block Printing block for reproducing line illustrations. Face of metal is solid, without any halftone or screen.

Line chart Two-dimensional diagram showing relationship between two different sets of data.

Liquidation Legal process bringing the life of a company to an end.

Liquidity Extent to which a company has available cash resources to meet its obligations.

Literal Typographical error requiring correction before printing commences.

Lithography Form of printing process from a flat as opposed to a raised surface. Ink impression is obtained by chemical treatment of surface such that certain areas retain ink whilst others reject it.

Live customers Active customers who are still trading and likely to continue trading with any particular company.

Live programme Performance and broadcast transmitted simultaneously.

Livery Distinctive dress or appearance of staff, equipment and communications of a particular company. *See* House style.

Local press Local newspapers, usually covering a borough or rural district. Published once or twice a week. *See* Provincial press.

Logotype Commonly used to describe a company symbol, badge or name style.

London Association for the Protection of Trade Organization providing status reports on credit-worthiness of companies within the London area.

London Gazette Weekly bulletin published with acknowledged authority in which the appearance of announcements makes them official.

Long-range plan Quantitative plan of development for the future, usually at least five years. *See* Corporate planning.

Loose inserts Advertisements distributed separately with a publication, and usually inserted loosely within its pages. *See* Insert.

Loss leader Product offered at cost price or less to increase store traffic.

Lost order reports Reports explaining why particular orders – usually contracts – have not been obtained or renewed.

Low pressure selling Concentration on winning customers' confidence and respect for long-term gains rather than gaining one particular order. Sometimes known as soft selling.

Lower case Printing convention designating small letters, as against capital letters, which are referred to as upper case.

Loyalty factor Supposition that the more a periodical is read the more likely it is that its readers will pay attention to its contents.

M

Magazine (1) Periodical, usually published weekly or monthly, and catering for special interest groups. (2) Container used to feed supplies into a mechanism, e.g. slide-projector.

Magnetic film Generic term for film coated with substance capable of retaining magnetic variations transferred to it by a magnetic head on a recorder. Used for the sound or audio input for a film, for example.

Magnetic sound track Sound track recorded on

magnetic tape, in much the same way as on a domestic tape recorder.

Magnetic tape Usually plastic strip coated with magnetic recording medium. *See* Magnetic film.

Mailing list Classified list of names and addresses suitable for distributing mailing shots. May be purchased or built up over time but requires careful maintenance to keep in an up-to-date condition.

Mailing piece Letter, leaflet or other article sent through the post on a widespread basis. *See* Direct mail.

Mailing shot Single mailing operation. Two mailings to the same list would be referred to as a two-shot campaign. *See* Direct mail shot.

Mail order Distribution channel. Customers buy direct by post either in response to an advertisement or from a sales promotional catalogue. Deliveries are made through the mail, by carrier direct from warehouse or factory, or sometimes through a local agent.

Make-good Repeating advertisement without charge, or refunding fee, due to error in advertisement as published.

Make-up Arrangement of type and plates in page form for advertising.

Management audit Systematic assessment of all management functions and techniques to establish the current level of effectiveness, and to lay down standards for future performance.

Management by objectives System whereby each management function is required to define the objectives each is set to achieve. Such objectives are designed to inter-relate for maximum efficiency, and require an effective feedback system to enable management to be aware of progress and to exercise adequate control.

Management development Deliberate formulation of plans to train staff and encourage them to acquire new skills in order to provide an organization with future executives, whilst at the same time giving staff a sense of purpose.

Manifest   Detailed list of a ship's cargo. This is sent to Customs officials within six days of clearance outwards.

Man profile   Specification of human characteristics, experience and training suited to the satisfactory performance of a particular job function. Usually formulated after the production of a job specification which similarly specifies the duties to be carried out.

Manual   Printed document (of any number of pages) usually containing specific instructions, e.g. sales manual, operating or service manual, relative both to products and services as well as company policies, regulations and practices.

Manufacturer's agent   Freelance sales agent employed by one or more manufacturers, usually on a 'commission on sales' basis, because of established connections in a particular market.

Margin   Normally the mark-up given to the cost price of a product by a distributor to cover his own costs and include some level of profit. Is sometimes referred to as the difference between the arbitrary cost of a product and the actual selling price.

Market   (1) Group of persons and/or organizations identified through a common need and with resources to satisfy that need. (2) Place where buyers and sellers gather to do business. (3) To market; to indulge in trade, i.e. buying and selling for pecuniary advantage.

Market attrition   Gradual wearing away of brand loyalty over time especially in the absence of promotional stimulus.

Market overt   Refers to an accepted convention whereby sellers of goods which are exposed in bulk, and part of normal stock in trade, may pass a good title for goods, irrespective of the title of the seller.

Market penetration Measures the extent to which market potential has been realized by companies supplying a market.

Market potential Estimated size of total present or future market. Alternatively, the maximum share of a market which can be reasonably achieved during a defined period.

Market price Price ruling for a commodity in the market place. Stated by economists as the value which a purchaser places upon a product or service to satisfy his need. Related to the Law of Marginal Utility.

Market profile Facts about members of a particular market group sufficient to identify such members.

Market reach Total number of prospects it is possible to reach through a given campaign.

Market research Process of making investigations into the characteristics of given markets, e.g. location, size, growth potential and observed attitudes. *See* Marketing research.

Market sales potential Calculation of cumulative sales value potential of a pre-determined market, taking into account different purchasing scales of preference.

Market share Percentage measure of the share obtained by an individual company from the total market available. Usually calculated upon a national basis but some international measures are in use.

Market weight Used for weighting advertising expenditure; means of varying expenditure according to the pattern of consumption by different market groups.

Marketing Marketing is still the subject of much misunderstanding, for it is not just a phenomenon of the twentieth century but a whole family of phenomena. The 'father' arose many centuries ago at the very beginning of trading, when merchants recognized the commercial advantages of supplying the food and clothing people needed, leaving others to minister to the needs of their souls. The 'mother' may be seen as a characteristic of the nineteenth and twentieth centuries. Using the fast-developing network of communications systems, the activities of marketing, the so-called marketing mix, joined with the already traditional 'concept of marketing' giving rise to the large family of today. It is in fact the confusion in identifying such offspring that antagonizes most non-marketing executives. For, although they spring from the same seed and share the same philosophies, the branches of the marketing family tree have reached different degrees of maturity and, like all children, have formed their own unique characteristics. So the practice of marketing in each branch of the family shows a markedly different profile. The branches are: Consumer goods marketing, Industrial goods marketing, Services marketing, International marketing, and Mini-marketing. Each of these areas of marketing practice has used the principles most applicable to its own market – true market orientation. It follows that various definitions of marketing tend to show the significance of one particular aspect, according to the branch in which the emphasis has been placed. Clearly, there are many definitions each of importance, yet different in substance. Some of these which endeavour to cover all facets of the subject are listed below for general guidance, though they here represent hundreds of attempts to provide a satisfactory explanation:

(1) The management process responsible for identifying, anticipating and satisfying customer requirements profitably. (Institute of Marketing definition 1975).
(2) Fundamental policy-forming activity devoted to selecting and developing suitable products for sale – promoting and distributing these products in a manner providing the optimum return on capital employed. (*Teach Yourself Marketing*, John Stapleton, 1975).

(3) Marketing starts in the market place with the identification of the customers' need. It then moves on to determining a means of satisfying that need, and of promoting, selling and supplying a satisfaction. The principal marketing functions might be defined as Marketing Information and Research, Product Planning, Advertising and Promotion, Sales and Distribution. (*Industrial Publicity*, Norman Hart, 1975).

Whatever the definition, it is clear that marketing is a positive business activity which establishes, develops, and satisfies both customer needs and wants. It is an intercommunications link provided by suppliers with a view to matching adequate supply with realistic demand, the reward for which is the operation of a profitable undertaking. It involves groups of commercial activities in contact with customers, and a concept permitting every critical business decision to be taken allowing for its present and future impact upon customers and society.

Marketing boards Producers' organizations established in UK under the provisions of the Marketing Acts in order to achieve an orderly supply and marketing of produce. They sometimes have assistance from public funds and provision is made for the protection of consumers.

Marketing mix Planned mixture of the elements of marketing in a marketing plan. The aim is to combine them in such a way as to achieve the greatest effect at minimum cost.

Marketing research Any research activity which provides information relating to marketing operations. Whilst the term embraces conventional market research, motivation studies, advertisement attention value, packaging effectiveness, logistics, and media research are also included, as well as analysis of internal and external statistics of relevance.

Marketing services   Term sometimes used to cover all marketing activities in a company other than the sales function, e.g. marketing research, advertising and public relations.

Marketing strategy   Written plan, usually comprehensive, describing all activities involved in achieving a particular marketing objective, and their relationship to one another in both time and magnitude. Will include short- and long-term sales forecasts, production and profit targets, pricing policy, promotional and selling strategy, staffing requirements, as well as the selected marketing mix and expense budgets.

Markov chain   Mathematical term describing a series of events in which each event is dependent upon the outcome of the previous event for its own particular result.

Mark-up   Amount added to a purchase price to provide a selling price. *See* Margin.

Married print   Visual and sound track made separately are 'married' by printing the two films onto one track.

Mass communications   Delivery of message to target audience utilizing mass media such as national press and television.

Mass media   Principally, television, radio and newspapers, i.e. those channels of communication which reach a very large market.

Master sample   Assembly of sampling points maintained by a number of research establishments and used as a basis for final selection of samples. This practice eliminates the expensive selection processes which would otherwise be required each time a survey or research study is commissioned.

Masthead Main heading or title at the top of a newspaper or magazine.

Matched sample Describes a technique wherein two or more samples with matching characteristics are used to provide realistic comparisons on different test subjects.

Matrix (1) Paper or plastic mould from which duplicate printing blocks are produced. (2) Horizontal and vertical lines or columns used for establishing relationships between sets of data.

MEAL (Media Expenditure Analysis Limited) Independent company which provides (for a fee) media expenditure analysis and statistics. *See* Legion.

Mean Arithmetic average where a total of distinct values is related to the number and distribution of each value to arrive at a figure intended to be representative of all the values. *See* Average.

Mean audit date Date at which the average shop in a retail audit sample was visited for the purpose of a particular report.

Measure In printing, length of line to which type is set.

Mechanical sales talk Continual use of trite expressions or cliches; often contained within the company sales or technical literature. Hence, sometimes described as 'canned' talk or presentation.

Media analyst Advertising agency worker (usually) employed to maintain and collate media statistics.

Media buyer Executive in an advertising agency, responsible for timely and economical purchasing of media time and space (readership or audience) to discharge the requirements of a client's media schedule.

Media commission Commission allowed by publishers and television contractors to 'recognized' advertising agencies in consideration of the space or time they book on behalf of their clients. *See* Recognition.

Media data form Established format for presenting data regarding a publication so as to facilitate comparison, particularly of circulation and rates. Also availabe for exhibitions.

Media planner Executive in an advertising agency responsible for formulating plans involving all types of media in such a way as to enable a client to reach out to his potential market(s) with maximum efficiency and minimum expense.

Media research Investigation and analysis of media, comprising:

(1) Media characteristics; (2) Qualitative factors; (3) Quantitative factors; (4) Cost factors; (5) Mechanical data.

In practice, is largely concerned with readership, audience and circulation data.

Media schedule Chart drawn up by an advertiser, usually with the aid of an advertising agency, setting out the media to be used in a campaign indicating the weight, timing and cost of each item.

Media-weight Used for weighting advertising expenditure; means of varying expenditure or actual decision criteria according to the value of particular media characteristics, especially the qualitative factors. It reflects the effectiveness with which an advertisement will work in a particular medium or publication.

Median Midpoint of a series of numerical data. Often referred to as a kind of average. Observed by inspection, e.g. 4, 7, 13, 16, 20; median is 13. Where the number of items in a series is even, interpolation may be used.

Medium Channel of communication, e.g. press organ, television station, exhibition or direct mail. Plural form is media, often used to refer specifically to periodical publications. *See* Advertising medium. *See also* Mass media.

Merchandising All activity directed towards selling goods once they have reached the point-of-sale, e.g. packaging, display, pricing, special offers. May be carried out by supplier's salesmen, store staff or jointly operated.

Merchantable quality Implied condition that a reasonable person would, after examination, accept goods as satisfactory to complete a contract for their purchase or sale.

Merger Amalgamation of two or more organizations with the object of growth, possibly to improve spending efficiency or to improve market performance but also to absorb competition. Mergers may be referred in UK to the Monopolies Commission for approval and are now increasingly affected by EEC regulations concerned with practices in restraint of trade. See Sections 85 and 86 of Treaty of Rome.

Merit rating Practice of ranking salesmen or other employees for payment or advancement according to their observed ability or achievement.

Milline rate Unit for comparing newspaper advertising rates in relation to circulation.

Minimil Lowest milline rate or an average of the lowest milline rates.

Minor Person not eligible to sign binding contracts, not having reached a majority (eighteen years in UK).

Misrepresentation Inducing another party to engage in a contract upon the basis of false or inadequate information.

Misrepresentation Act 1967 Under this Act, compensation may be obtained, even for innocent misrepresentation, unless the seller can prove information was truly represented in terms of fact(s), opinion(s) not being acceptable in lieu of fact(s).

Missionary salesman Salesman calling, for example, upon a doctor, who is not a purchasing agent, so as to promote goodwill in an effort to stimulate sales through prescriptions to a third party, the patient, who is supplied by a chemist. *See* Propaganda selling.

Mixed economy National economy with elements of both publicly-owned industries and private enterprise industries, operating side-by-side. Public undertakings enjoy a large measure of monopoly power, protected by law, whereas private monopolies are banned or restricted.

Mobility Freedom with which labour, or other resources, move to other uses in an economy.

Mock-up Facsimile of package or product for use in photography for television or other visual display form. *See* Dummy.

Mode Most commonly recurring value(s) in any recorded numerical data. Such clusters are often referred to as averages and may sometimes be more representative of the data than the arithmetic mean.

Model (1) Mathematical representation of real life situation. (2) Person used to illustrate an advertisement. (3) Reproduction on a small scale.

Modification In product development, to change a product or its presentation in order to effect improvement in performance, characteristics, acceptability, manufacturing procedure, or profitability.

Monadic Single product test. Used as a test of acceptance or validity as an alternative to a comparative assessment.

Money Any acceptable means of settling debts as an established practice within a nation or group of nations. *See* Legal tender.

Monitor To check performance at regular intervals in relation to pre-established norms.

Monopolistic competition   State said by economists to exist when a restricted number of firms compete not so much by price and performance as by competitive promotional outlays. Products are thus differentiated in the market place by the amount of pressure generated upon demand rather than by any significant differences between them.

Monopoly   (1) Sole producer or supplier to person or organization of a commodity or service. (2) In UK, private companies are referred to the Monopolies Commission if they account for more than a percentage of the total national output of their product. This proportion was reduced by law to 25% from 1975. Publicly-owned (nationalized) industries industries are exempted from such provisions.

Mood advertising   Advertising which is deliberately aimed at putting potential customers into a frame of mind conducive to acceptance of the product.

Motivation   Psychological stimulus behind the acts or courses of action adopted by individuals or groups of individuals. Applied in marketing both to individual and organizational activities as well as to consumer and user behaviour.

Motivational research   Study of psychological reasons underlying human behaviour particularly in relation to buying situations. *See* Group discussion.

Mould   *See* Matrix.

Moving average   Statistical technique used for reducing the significance of wide seasonal or other variations. Moves forward on a periodical basis, (e.g. every week or month by adding the most recent data and dropping the oldest). A smoothing technique to permit longer term trends to be more clearly discerned. *See* Experimental smoothing.

Multiple   Group of shops with similar merchandise and image and controlled by a single firm.

Multiple readership   More than one reader per issue,

D

usually involving secondary and tertiary readers. In trade and technical press, can amount to double figures for each copy.

Multiplier (1) Keynes' term for the phenomenon of a total increase in national income being several times greater than an initial injection of investment in a community. (2) Ratio in investment designed to produce a given increase in employment.

Multi-stage sample Sample assembled by combining proportionate numbers of respondents of different characteristics represented in a universe. Selection is random within each category. Satisfactorily combines the benefits of both quota and random sampling.

Multivariate analysis Technique used for assessing the extent to which variables cause a number of differences in subsequent behaviour patterns.

N

National Freight Corporation Created under the Transport Act, 1968 to promote properly integrated services for the carriage of goods either by road or rail within Great Britain and, where economic and efficient, to ensure the proper utilization of rail services. The Corporation also provides carriage services abroad, storage, harbours, hovercraft and vehicles on hire. It is not a common carrier. It controls British Road Services Ltd., British Roadtrailer Services Ltd., Pickfords Ltd., Tartan Arrow Services (Holdings) Ltd., and Transport Holding Company Trustees Ltd.

National Marketing Council Established in 1965 by British Productivity Council with committees whose aim was to spread knowledge, nationally and internationally, about modern marketing techniques. Since dissolved; co-ordination now being administered by the Advertising Association through the informal Committee of Marketing Organizations (COMO).

National press Newspapers, daily or Sunday, distributed throughout the country but not necessarily enjoying a mass circulation.

Negotiations Seeking agreement on mutually acceptable terms prior to concluding a trading agreement.

Net audience Number of unduplicated homes, readers or viewers, etc, also known as net readership.

Net price Final price after all discounts and allowances have been deducted.

Net rate Publisher's rates after deduction of agency commission.

Net reach Number of people who will have at least one opportunity to see an advertisement after allowing for duplication of readership between issues and between publication.

Netting Plastic netting extruded as a continuous cylinder and chopped into single units which are used to hold units of merchandise and to enhance their display. Frequently used for fruit or vegetable display in self-service stores.

Network Television or radio stations linked together for transmitting identical programmes simultaneously. Refers also to the facility by which programmes may be retransmitted by other TV regions, and thus similar to syndicated press features.

Network analysis Breaking down a complex project into component requirements and recording these in a diagramatic form which incorporates a critical time scale, so that planning and control can be effected in the most expedient manner.

Newsprint Coarse paper from which newspapers are commonly produced.

News release *See* Press release.

Next-to-reading matter Advertisement position immediately adjacent to editorial. *See* Facing matter.

Nominal price Face value of an item, often used to indicate a minor charge being made for something of greater economic value.

Normal distribution Statistical term central to sampling theory. On a line chart, it shows the point at which the mean, mode, and median averages share the same value and has a characteristic bell-shaped profile. Standard deviation is calculated upon a formula derived from this distribution, enabling the confidence level (e.g. 95%) within which results are confined to be stated. In the example given, this would be accuracy defined to within $\pm$ 5%.

Noting Term used in advertisement research. Indicates that a reader's attention was drawn to an advertisement when first looking through the newspaper or magazine in which it appeared, though not necessarily that he read, fully understood or acted upon this stimulus.

Noting score Average number of readers found to have noted a specific advertisement or editorial item expressed as a percentage of total readership.

NRS (National Readership Survey) Survey conducted under the auspices of JICNARS, to determine the readership of major national newspapers and consumer magazines in UK.

Numerical concentration Selection of the most economic or effective media based on readership figures which most closely match those of the chosen target audience, after duplication and wasted readership have been eliminated.

O

Objection, overcoming Anticipating likely forms of sales resistance, reacting to an objection and providing real or, at least, plausible answers. These objections are sometimes, if not frequently, contrived to provide a camouflage for the real reasons which the prospect may not care to disclose to a stranger. Hence the importance of a salesman's technique in identifying and dealing with the real situation.

Objective selling Selling against predetermined aims, e.g. to obtain an interview or a demonstration, where an immediate sale is not always possible.

Obsolescence Indicative of a significant relative decline in a product's usefulness or competitiveness in the market. This occurs when alternative products become available which have a better performance or lower price. The final stage before a product finally becomes obsolete. The phrase 'planned obsolescence' refers to the adoption of a policy of relatively frequent design changes to induce users to renew their equipment more often than would otherwise be the case, e.g. motor cars.

Obsolescent product Product no longer representing current production.

Offer Legally, the first step in the making of a contract for the sale (or acquisition) of goods.

Off peak time All airtime segments (television and radio) other than those occurring at peak time. Usually offered at significantly lower rates.

Offset-litho Offsetting is merely that part of the process by which the image on a litho plate is transferred to a rubber sheet which then prints onto paper, thus avoiding a mirror or reversed reproduction. *See* Lithography.

Oligopoly Influence exercised over a market supply by

only a small number of independent companies, not necessarily acting in collusion.

Omnibus Continuous survey which is used to cover a number of topics at the same time. Companies offering this facility invite sponsors to commission a limited number of questions which would not alone justify setting up a separate research study.

One-stop shopping Facility to provide shoppers with a wide range of goods from one, often covered, shopping centre, usually with parking facilities. Frequently in UK a municipal enterprise as opposed to Hypermarkets and Supermarkets operated by private firms.

On-pack price reductions Price cut, such as '3p off' printed on pack as a temporary promotional device aimed at securing trial purchases and increasing market penetration.

Open-ended question Formulation of question in a field research which allows respondents to provide a reply in their own terms, i.e. uninfluenced by guidance within the questionnaire or upon the part of the interviewer.

Open pricing General circulation of pricing practices with a view to achieving conformity of prices within an industry.

Operational research Application of mathematical processes to operational problems, having the effect of increasing the proportion of factual data, especially its use in helping to resolve questions which are essentially subjective in its absence.

Opportunity cost Value of an opportunity to use committed funds in an alternative way.

Order Instruction to supply goods or services. *See* Quotation. *See also* Contract.

Order/call ratio Relationship between the number of orders obtained and the number of calls made to get them over a particular period of operation. Establishes a useful comparative tool for sales efficiency supervision.

Organization and methods Examination of the structure of an organization, its management and control, its procedures and methods and their comparative efficiency in achieving organizational objectives.

Opinion formers Groups or categories of people who, because of their status or position, are considered to exert more than usual influence on the views of others.

OTS (Opportunities to see) A measure published by media owners. The figure shown always represents the average OTS for the audience reached.

Outdoor advertising Mainly poster and transport advertising, but including illuminated signs and outdoor displays.

Outer pack Container which holds a number of units and whose function usually is one of protection during distribution. It may also be used to carry an advertising message.

Outside broadcast Television programme transmitted from a particular location and not from the studio.

Overcoming objections *See* Objection, overcoming.

Overlap Normally refers to those areas of the country which are covered by two or more ITV transmitters, e.g. South London where both London and Southern programmes can be received.

Overlay Transparent or translucent sheet of paper laid over one piece of artwork carrying further artwork which is to be reproduced in a different colour; or for protection; or to facilitate instructions on how it should be used or modified for production.

Overmatter Excess of type in printing, in relation to the space available.

Overselling (1) Persuading distributor or customer to

order more goods than they can reasonably handle or
consume. (2) Overstating the case for buying a product or
service.

Overtrading Transacting more business than working
capital will allow to be serviced and thereby producing
serious strains upon cash flow, due to the lag in payment by
customers subsequent to the placing of orders.

Own label Branding of products by the outlet itself
rather than the manufacturer or distributor. Used widely
by chain stores and supermarkets for goods usually sold at
lower prices than nationally advertised branded
alternatives in an effort to maintain customer loyalty.

P

Pack (package, packet) The product of a complete
series of packaging operations or a unit consisting of a
number of such products (BS 3130).

Packaging (1) The art of and the operations involved in
the preparation of articles or commodities for carriage,
storage, and delivery (BS 3130). (2) Marketing communications channel.

Packing The operations of packaging by which articles
or commodities are enveloped in wrapping and/or enclosed
in containers or otherwise secured (BS 3130).

Packing case Usually applied to a case constructed of
soft timber for the protection of goods in transit, a common
precaution in the case of heavy goods and export
shipments.

Page exposure *See* Page traffic.

Page proofs Proofs of a leaflet, brochure, magazine or
book, taken at the stage when the pages have been made up
and used for final review and correction before printing is
commenced.

Page traffic   Number of readers of a particular page in a publication expressed as a percentage of the total readership of that publication. *See* Read most. *See also* Noting.

Pagination   Numbering of pages in a printed publication. *See* Folio.

Pallet   Platform, usually of timber, upon which units are stacked, e.g. fibreboard cases, for bulk movement and transportation. Designed to be used in conjunction with fork-lift trucks.

Pan/panning   Abbreviation from panorama; slow movement of camera from left to right, or vice versa, across a scene, with camera set-up remaining stationary.

Panel   Sample of retail establishments or consumers specially recruited to provide information on buying, media, and consumption habits and sometimes to test potential new products. Requires careful supervision and maintenance to preserve effective data basis.

Pantry check   Used in connection with a panel to establish what is available in the home for consumption and as a check upon the veracity of reportage.

Paper   Sheet material manufactured mostly from woodpulp and used in printing and packaging in a variety of grades, e.g. Kraft, a very tough paper for bags and sacks; glassine, a specially processed paper which is grease resistent.

Paperboard   Commonly known as cardboard. Comprises a number of layers of wood fibres, sometimes of differing qualities, which are bonded together during their formation on a board machine.

Paper setting   Setting of an advertisement by the printer of a periodical, usually free of charge. *See* Trade setting.

Parallel readership   Reduction of the average claim period for readership research, where a second reading event occurs during original claim period so introducing error into estimated average readership figures leading to understatement of readership. *See* Readership replication.

Parameter (1) A quantity whose value specifies or partly specifies the process under consideration or the values of other quantities (BS 3527). (2) A quantity which changes relatively infrequently during a computation; in particular, in a routine, a quantity which may be given a different value each time the routine is used, but which remains unchanged throughout any one routine. (BS 3527).

Pareto effect (or law) Operates where a small proportion has a disproportionate effect on the whole. Often used to refer to the so-called 80/20 rule, whereby 20% of customers may take 80% of production and vice versa. More commonly observed in industrial than in consumer goods marketing, though examples can be found in both sectors.

Part-load (1) Goods occupying an unfilled transport vehicle. (2) Part-order or delivery.

Partnership Association of limited number of persons carrying on business together, usually with a profit motive. Particularly associated with small or localized businesses with limited opportunities for expansion, e.g. professional undertakings such as dentists and solicitors.

Pass for press Final approval of a publication before printing.

Patronage Of consumers, habitual use of particular sources of supply. *See* Testimonial advertisement.

Patterned interview Technique of planned selling where interview is conducted by salesmen according to a predetermined plan.

Peak time Segment of television airtime, usually the middle part of the evening, where the highest rate is charged and, theoretically, the highest number of people are viewing. Has similar application in radio transmissions.

Peak time band   In television advertising, a span of time during which it can be forecast the maximum audience will be viewing. Potentially applicable to radio commercials.

Pedlars   Door-to-door or street salesmen carrying stock of wares or services for immediate sales on demand.

Penalty clause   Clause in an agreement stipulating compensation of an agreed amount (or some alternative course of action) upon breach of a contract. The penalty clause will not necessarily reflect the true cost of the breach, which may be difficult to estimate in advance of the event.

Penetration   Extent to which a product or an advertisement has been accepted by, or has registered with the total of possible users, usually expressed as a percentage.

Penetration pricing   Adoption of a lower price strategy in order to secure rapid wide penetration of a market.

Per capita income   Total income of a nation averaged over its population, thus giving an arbitrary but comparative measure of income per head of the population.

Perfect competition   Term used by economists to describe an open market situation, where free trade prevails without restriction, where all goods of a particular nature are homogeneous and where all relevant information is known to both buyers and sellers. Such conditions rarely, if ever, apply in fact but the hypothesis has been found useful in analysing the forces governing the operation of supply and demand factors in real life conditions.

Personal selling   The process of making oral commercial representations during a buyer/seller interview situation. Colloquially referred to as face-to-face selling. Sometimes known as buyer/seller interface.

107

Personality promotions (1) Use of well-known persons to endorse a product or service. *See* Testimonial advertising. (2) Use of readily identifiable, often gaily dressed, persons from whom a prize can be claimed if approached with the use of a promotional phrase or saying.

Persuasive communication Any form of communication which is primarily intended to exercise persuasion, e.g. advertising, editorial publicity, sales presentations, speeches, films and filmstrips, etc.

Phased or zonal distribution Distributing goods to one area or one group of customers at a time, until a national network has been established. *See* Zone.

Photogravure Printing process in which the subject matter is photochemically etched into a polished copper cylinder. Used widely for large-circulation colour magazines.

Pie chart Pictorial presentation, showing the parts of a total activity or performance as sectors of a circle. May also be used to contrast the behaviour of two sets of variables by comparing the angular dimensions and/or area of each piece and changes occurring over time.

Pied type Used by printers to describe words or lines of type rendered meaningless by displaced or wrong letters.

Pilot Test survey to check mechanical or operating details before embarking upon a major study.

Pioneer selling *See* Commando selling.

Pitch Colloquial term describing an agency presentation before a prospective client. Also refers to a sales pitch – a presentation by a salesman to a buyer. *See* Presentation.

Placement test In such a test, products or packs are delivered to selected usage points for trial to be followed up by interviews collecting information on performance and attitudes towards them. *See* Extended use tests.

Planned selling Operating selling activity along

predetermined lines with calculated aims and goals, specified strategies and tactics, and monitored against these standards; it means guiding and controlling each sales interview against a plan setting its objectives, yet allowing some degree of variations to occur in achieving them, reflecting the human situations involved but keeping salesman operation within a systematic schedule.

Plastics   Synthetic materials available in a variety of forms, sheeting, mouldings, extrusions and laminates. Have a wide range of properties, optical and mechanical, and are particularly resistent to water and to solvents and other chemicals. Available in rigid, semi-rigid, or pliable form. Basically of two types: thermoplastics (which soften or melt with heat), e.g. polyethylene, polyvinyl chloride (PVC), polystyrene; or thermosetting, which hardens (polymerizes) on the first application of heat, and thereafter maintain their form, e.g. phenol formaldehyde (Bakelite), urea formaldehyde. Some plastics can be 'blown' into expanded form with a variety of uses in packaging, e.g. foam plastic. *See* Blister pack.

Plate   Printing block or litho plate.

Playback   (1) Reproduction on closed circuit of recorded material. (2) Reproduction of material, either live or recorded, through a loudspeaker to enable actors to synchronize with it.

Plug   Promotion of product or company by medium without charge. Often used as a testimonial in conversation.

Point   (1) Unit of type – 0.0138 inches, 12 points to the pica, approximately 72 points to the inch. (2) Full-stop.

Point-of-purchase   Arguable alternative term to point-of-sale, but may differ in some respects, e.g. in mail order where the point-of-purchase differs from the point-of-sale in terms of time span, or where vending machines are in use.

Point-of-sale   Place at which a sale is made; also refers to publicity material used there, e.g. posters, showcards, display units, dispensers and leaflets.

Poll (1) Public opinion survey. (2) To seek information.

Population Total number in a group, whether geographical area or specialized group.

Portfolio Presentation kit used by salesman when interviewing prospective customers.

Postcall analysis Reviewing achievements following sales interview. *See* Kerbside conference.

Poster Placard displayed in public place.

Post Office (1) Individual or regional office used for relaying messages. (2) Public corporation providing services in telecommunications and mailing.

Pre-approach Preparation of all relevant material in relation to objectives prior to a selling interview.

Pre-coded Questions to be put and the possible answers which may be received in a survey are keyed to enable easy tabulation of results using a numerical coding system. This facilitates computer analysis making possible the rapid handling of a high volume of data.

Pre-empt spot In television, an advertisement spot bought in advance in a particular time segment at a discount but which will not be screened if another advertiser offers to take up that time at the full rate.

Preferred position Advertisement position in a publication against which a premium charge is made.

Premium Additional price charged in return for some commercial benefit over and above the product itself.

Premium offer Special offer of merchandise at a reduced price in consideration of purchasing a particular product, as evidenced by the sending in of a qualifying number of labels or coupons. Usually conducted as a self-liquidating operation.

Presence Refers to a form of measurement which endeavours to indicate whether members of a target audience are actually present during the transmission of commercials as well as the programmes within which they are slotted. Crude viewing figures require modification for translation in terms of attention value.

Presentation Meeting in which proposals are put to an audience in a planned and usually formal manner. Much used by advertising and research agencies but also used by companies communicating with distributors or, for example, publishers desiring to influence main opinion formers.

Press All periodicals, whether national, local, trade, or technical.

Press advertising Advertising in the press. *See* Advertising.

Press conference *See* Press reception.

Press cuttings Excerpts on a particular subject cut from any kind of periodical. Used as a monitoring device to indicate the extent to which a subject is receiving publicity.

Press date Date on which a publication or a section of a publication is due to be passed for press. *See* Copy date.

Press reception Meeting to which press representatives – editors, journalists, reporters – are invited in order to be informed of an event, and to have the opportunity of questioning or commenting.

Press relations That part of public relations activity aimed at establishing and maintaining a favourable relationship both with and through the press.

Press release Written statement describing an event or item which is considered to be of sufficient interest to readers for an editor to publish some reference to it. Sometimes referred to as a news release – a more appropriate term as it includes the use of broadcasting media.

Press visit   Visit by members of the press to a place of interest, usually coupled with a special event, such as the official opening of a new establishment or launching of a new activity.

Pressure selling   Forceful selling effort. Referred to as high pressure selling when the effort is perceived to be aggressive. *See* Low pressure selling.

Prestige advertising   *See* Corporate advertising.

Pre-test   Test of product or advertisement prior to full scale testing programme.

Pre-testing   *See* Product evaluation. *See also* Product testing; Concept testing.

Pre-testing copy   Exploratory research to check the efficacy of a particular piece of advertising copy prior to its being used in an actual advertisement.

Price   Agreed exchange value forming the essential basis for a trading agreement.

Price cutting   Selling at prices below the commonly accepted level for the product or commodity concerned.

Price-demand elasticity   Relationship between the selling price of a product and the volume of demand which will be generated as a result. High elasticity is indicative of a product for which demand will be very sensitive to changes in price. This is often to be found in highly competitive markets and is more closely associated with nonessential commodities. Low elasticity will apply to essentials and particularly in a monopolistic situation. Price-demand elasticity should never be taken to imply that reducing prices will inevitably lead to increasing demand or that increasing prices will result in a reduction in demand; the reverse may actually occur in both cases. *See* Giffen goods.

Price discrimination   Charging different prices to

different markets or classes of buyers. Occurs most commonly as between cash and credit or instalment purchases but will also reflect the value of particular outlets.

Price/earnings ratio   Quoted price of an ordinary share divided by the most recent year's earnings per share.

Price index   Sequence of price changes expressed against a base year, usually starting at 100. *See* Indexing.

Price mechanism   System of allocation of scarce resources according to effective demand, expressed through price and price movements.

Pricing plateau   Round figure for selling price, above and below which sharply increasing elasticity tends to occur, hence fixing of price at £4.99 rather than £5.

Price structure   Detailed prices and discounts, the amount of detail depending on whether prepared for trade or the final user or consumer.

Pricing strategy   Deliberate planning of the pricing structure in relation to factors such as consumer wants, product attributes and competition in such a way as to ensure overall profitability. Such a strategy must have regard to price-demand elasticity as well as encompassing such variables and incentives as volume discounts, commission and premium offers.

Pricing tactics   Short-term pricing manipulation used in an effort to stimulate brand switching or an increase in the share of total market.

Primary readership   Readership figures based upon initial purchasers of a publication, e.g. paid for by any member of a household. *See* Secondary readership. *See also* Tertiary readership.

Private carrier   Carries goods according to specific contracts and is under no obligation to provide scheduled services.

Probability Basis of sampling theory; providing sufficient history of an event is known, then the probability that it will occur again is calculable.

Probe Used to obtain further information when the initial inquiry does not produce a satisfactory response, or to make sure at interview that the respondent has answered the question fully.

Product benefits Factors which go towards satisfying the requirements of a customer. Fundamentally, the purchasing decision is based upon the perceived product benefits rather than the product itself or its specification or performance. *See* Consumer want.

Product development Activity leading to a product having new or different characteristics or consumer benefits. Such developments range from an entirely new concept to meet a newly defined consumer 'want' to the modification of an existing product or indeed its presentation and packaging. It forms part of a process which has to be continuous to arrest the decline era within the intrinsic life cycle of any existing product.

Product development cycle Chain of events leading up to the birth of a new product, i.e. concept, mock-up, prototype, preproduction batch, full production.

Product evaluation Of particular relevance to new products, product evaluation is the means by which the value of a product to a customer is determined in advance. This is of special importance in developing a pricing strategy but, in practice, should go much deeper in order to categorize each of the product benefits in relation to each of the market segments. From such essential background knowledge develops not only the marketing strategy and the media mix, but also the basic selling platform and the advertising appropriation.

Production Term used essentially in advertising and

referring to the process of putting into a reproductive form illustrations or words with a view to printing, e.g. block making, typesetting, or scripting for transmission. Also applied to the management of all mechanical processes required to achieve the reproduction of an advertising message. Sometimes referred to within an agency as 'traffic control'.

Product life cycle *See* Life cycle.

Product mix Range of products which, when viewed as a whole, provides a more than proportionate return than the sum of the individual items if marketed in isolation. Such a return can be achieved by adding complementary products to an existing range and sold to the same market without significant additional expense. Alternatively, existing products with minor modifications involving little further expense can find a demand in different market segments. A product mix can be such that seasonal demands for one are offset by those of another, thereby maintaining continuity of production and distribution resources. Yet again, the mix can be so structured as to embrace products in each of the stages of the product life cycle. *See* Synergy.

Product performance Relates to the intrinsic attributes of a product. These may not necessarily be in line with its specification, nor, for that matter, the requirements of all potential customers; cf. the Anglo-French Concorde.

Product/price parity Near homogeneous products at identical prices.

Product testing Anonymous product testing and product evaluation. *See* evaluation.

Product, weighted distribution Distribution weighted to allow for the known disproportionate influences in different outlets. Weights will usually be determined by relative significance of factors, e.g. level of purchasing power or areas of light or heavy usage, e.g. of 'hard' or 'soft' water.

Profile Detailed description of subject, often a person, or groups of subjects. Sometimes expressed as percentages against predetermined criteria, intended to make identification of the subject, perhaps the target user or consumer, readily possible.

Profit Often used to describe the surplus resulting after a defined trading period but must be regarded as the first essential charge upon a business, being a reward for engaging resources in conditions of speculative risk for the satisfaction of consumer demand. It furnishes resources to invest in future operations and consequently its absence must result in a decline in effective capital resources and ultimately competitive extinction of the business.

Profit centre Application of responsibility accounting to a unit or centre of activity through which profits are accrued.

Pro forma invoice Document stating the value of a transaction used to notify the proposed despatch of a consignment of goods. It is frequently used as a means of obtaining prepayment or of permitting the buyer to obtain exchange control sanction for the necessary remittance from another country.

Progressives Set of proofs taken from the individual blocks or plates constituting a four-colour set for the purpose of checking clarity and correct alignment. *See* Four-colour set.

Projection (1) Forecasting process (extrapolation) using trends in a time series to estimate future values. (2) Psychological research technique to identify true attitudes, for example, towards a product, rather than the socially acceptable reasons which may be put forward by respondents.

Prompt (1) Providing a number of alternative answers in a questionnaire to enable a respondent to select the one most appropriate to his/her beliefs. (2) Mastheads or

magazine covers used in readership research to help
respondents remember the titles they have read, or the
product they have seen advertised.

Proof Preliminary printing, usually by a manual
process, to facilitate checking and approval prior to final
mechanical printing. *See* Block pull.

Propaganda selling *See* Missionary selling.

Pro rata freight Proportion of freight charges due as a
result of cargo being delivered to a port short of the port of
destination.

Prospect Potential purchaser of a given product or
service.

Prototype First working model or initially constructed
version of a product. To all intents and purposes, the
prototype is the product in appearance, characteristics and
performance. Its existence facilitates numerous judg-
ments, tests and management decisions regarding future
developments.

Provincial press Newspapers, circulating daily or
weekly in a restricted geographic region, e.g. a city or
county. Otherwise referred to as local press or regional
press.

Pseudo product testing In which the same basic
product is presented in a variety of ways, e.g. different
packs, to a test group who are asked to give a preference
rating. This determines customers' capability of discerning
differences, or lack of them, and gives an indication of the
virtues of each form of presentation.

Psychogalvanometer Measuring device used in
advertising research to determine the emotional effect of
advertising messages by reaction to the rate of perspiration
flow exhibited by the viewer.

Psychographics A technique devoted to the

segmentation of markets using psychological criteria to distinguish between the different segments.

Psychology of selling Explanation of the sales process which lays emphasis upon the workings of psychological factors and particularly their manipulation by salesmen to secure a favourable response to their propositions.

Publication date Officially stated date when a publication becomes available for purchase or distribution.

Public relations Conscious effort to improve and maintain an organization's relationships with such publics as employees, customers, shareholders, local communities, trade unions. Not to be confused with Press relations.

Public relations consultant Individual or firm employed by an organization to advise and/or act on its behalf in the field of public relations.

Public relations officer Executive responsible for planning and implementing the public relations policy of an organization.

Publicity Process of securing public attention for messages to be imparted. *See* Advertising; Public relations; and Sales promotion – all of which fall to some extent within the category indicated by this term.

Publicity manager Person responsible for managing a company's publicity. *See* Advertising manager.

Publics Public relations terminology describing groups of people which can readily be identified as having some special relevance to a business or other organization, e.g. customers, employees, shareholders, suppliers and the local community generally.

Publisher's statement Statement by a publishing company of the circulation and other information relating to a particular publication. Not necessarily independently audited. *See* ABC.

Publishing Business of producing books, magazines,

newspapers, and other periodicals, and distributing them to the public via bookshops, newsagents, mail or other outlets.

Puff   Reference by individual or organization, usually in the media, to a product or company with the intention of providing favourable publicity.

Pull   *See* Block pull.

Punnet   Specialized paperboard carton, or wooden container, open to inspection of contents and used principally for dispensing soft fruit by weight.

Purchasing agent/officer   Representative of buying firm group. *See* Buyer (1) and (2).

Purchasing motives   *See* Buying motives.

Purchasing power   Extent to which an organization, group of people or a geographical area with funds available, whether committed or otherwise, has the ability to make purchases during specified time periods.

Pyramid selling   Form of franchising where personnel are recruited against financial standards of entry and help to establish a distribution network of commission agents. System became almost unworkable from 1973 following parliamentary action to restrain its further development in Britain.

Q

Quad crown   Poster size equal to two double crowns. *See* Double crown.

Qualitative research   Deals with data frequently difficult to quantify; often expressed as value judgements by individuals from which any collective general conclusions are difficult to draw. Such research usually involves group discussions or interviews.

Quality control Important procedure usually involving the random inspection of goods with a view to maintaining specified standards.

Quantitative research Research findings which may be expressed numerically. They may then be subjected to mathematical or statistical manipulation to produce forecasts of future events under differing environmental conditions.

Quasi contracts While no actual contract exists, the courts would hold on such a basis that one party nevertheless has an obligation towards another.

Queen's Award to Industry Annual awards made on 21 April in recognition of outstanding achievement by firms in exporting or in technological innovation.

Questionnaire Base document for research studies which provides the questions and the structure for an interview and has provision for respondents' answers. Requires considerable skill in design, involving understanding of human nature and communication processes.

Quota (1) Structure of a sample specifying number and type of persons required for interviews. (2) Sales target figure for salesman that may be expressed as required minimum performance or act as threshold for commission payment.

Quota sample Preselected groups for interviewing, constructed so as to represent the known characteristics of the whole population.

Quotation Specific offer, verbal or written, of goods or services, the acceptance of which will form a contract.

R

Random sample Statistical term specifying the situation in which each possible informant within the population has an equal choice of selection. In practice to reduce the costs involved, quota sampling technique may be used for initial processing of possible informants and random selection techniques would be applied at the final stages.

Rate card Document issued by publishers or advertising contractors showing the charges made for various types and sizes of advertisement and including the relevant mechanical data to govern advertisement production.

Rating Applied especially to broadcasting media and meaning the relative audience or viewership achieved by a programme or advertisement, as compared with others, e.g. a popularity rating. Used also in research studies. *See* TVR.

Rationalization In reference to products, the elimination of items in the range which bring in the minimum return and call for a disproportionate effort to sustain demand. Rationalization leads to a concentration of resources into those products from which a maximum return can be expected.

Reach Synonym for cumulative audience.

Reader involvement Copywriting with the aim of gaining the participation of the reader; a particular facet of local newspapers and radio.

Reader service card *See* Bingo card.

Readership Number of people who read a publication as opposed to the number of people included in its circulation. *See* Circulation.

Readership replication Extension of the claim period for readership research where a second reading event occurs during or after original claim period, so introducing error into estimated readership figures, leading to overestimation of readership. *See* Parallel readership.

Reading and noting Readership research index of

actual audience for advertisements appearing on particular pages or average pages in specific publications. *See* Page traffic.

Read most Term used in assessing the effectiveness of an advertisement in the press. Respondents are asked to indicate whether, if they noted an advertisement, they then 'read most' of its copy. This data can then be expressed as a percentage of total readership.

Real income Income as expressed in terms of the goods and services it can purchase.

Rears Spaces available on the backs of buses for advertisement posters. Especially suitable for certain products, e.g. garages, motor tyres and spares, travel, and driving school services.

Recall (1) Spontaneous: where an informant's memory is allowed to suggest information without guidance or assistance. (2) Prompted (aided recall) or assisted memory, where informant is shown possible alternatives, or part of the actual subject matter, as a memory stimulus.

Reciprocal trading Arrangement between organizations whereby their roles as seller and buyer are interchangeable, i.e. they buy from and sell to each other. Commonly found between member companies of a group but also exists between independent firms where mutual interests may thus be economically served. *See* Transfer price.

Recognition (1) Method of testing effect of advertising. *See* Recall. (2) Advertising agencies apply to controlling media organizations (NPA, PPA, ARIC and ITCA) for recognition and are then entitled to receive commission from media owners. It is difficult for an agency to operate if denied this form of recognition, which is most frequently a credit-rating device but may also be used as a means of applying pressure to conform.

Recruitment advertising Advertising designed to

recruit staff of any kind. Consists mostly of classified and semi-display advertisements. *See* Display advertisement.

Redemption Process of trading in or redeeming coupons, vouchers, special offers, trading stamps and the like in exchange for a stated product or benefit.

Regional press *See* Provincial press.

Registered design Design which is legally registered thus providing protection against its unauthorized use by any other person or organization.

Regression analysis Mathematical technique for establishing the relationship between observed and quantifiable variables, both past and present.

Reminiscence Improvement in retention of factual data over time without further relevant communications. *See* Sleeper effect.

Repeat purchasing Products subject to frequent usage, usually of low unit value and bought regularly for habitual consumption. Convenience plays a large part in such purchasing and substitution will often occur if the preferred brand is not readily available, e.g. newspapers, tobacco, office supplies. *See* Convenience goods.

Reply card Used, for instance, in a direct mail campaign, in which a card is enclosed, usually prepaid, to encourage a reply. *See* Bingo card.

Reprint Copies of an advertisement printed after appearance in a publication.

Repro pulls Good quality proofs of typesetting, usually for use in making up artwork, or in enlarging for display purposes.

Resale price maintenance Agreement between trading concerns regarding prices at which goods may be sold. Prohibited in UK under the 1964 Resale Prices Act so that suppliers may now only publish a recommended retail price (RRP).

Reserve price   Minimum selling price. Most often used at auctions but may occasionally apply when stock is being cleared at reduced prices.

Respondent   Research informant. *See* Informant.

Response   Reaction evoked by a stimulus.

Response function   Set of numbers, often in percentage form, defining the relative value of given numbers of advertising impressions per person or section of the target population.

Response rate   Measure of advertising effectiveness, e.g. in direct mail, the number of replies per thousand; in other forms of advertising, the number of replies per insertion. Taken in conjunction with readership/viewership figures for example, this measure enables a comparative cost per inquiry structure to be compiled for use in media selection.

Retail audit   Study of preselected sample of retail outlets, providing information on the sales volume, sales trends, stock levels, display and promotional effectiveness of brands, the suppliers of which pay a subscription in return for the regular supply of such information.

Retailers' co-operatives   Retail buying groups owning and operating a wholesale facility for members and often selling under a common brand name. A common feature in agricultural marketing for sale of specific commodities to farmers and market gardeners.

Retiring a bill   Refers to a bill of exchange which is paid on its due date.

Retrospective analysis   Study of a situation after the event; colloquially referred to as 'post mortem'.

Returns   (1) Measure of income arising from an investment. (2) Applies to goods returned, damaged, unsatisfactory or surplus, to a supplier for credit.

Reverse plate Printing block in which the contents – illustrations and lettering – are in white upon a black or coloured background.

Right of resale Legal term to cover circumstances under which a seller of goods still in possession may resell goods, even though he may not hold title to them. Any surplus on the transaction accrues to the original supplier, after the expenses of the seller have been met.

Robot salesmen (1) Purely mechanical sales effort by salesmen. (2) Dispensing machines, vending machines.

Role playing Acting a part in a simulated face-to-face interview, usually at a sales meeting or training session.

Rotogravure *See* Photogravure.

Rough Illustration or design of a layout for an advertisement or other printwork in rough form. *See* Scamp.

Rough out First edited assembly of film shots in correct order and sequence according to script instructions.

Rounding off Mathematical procedure for eliminating small insignificant numbers or decimals of numbers, by taking the nearest significant value.

Routing salesmen Designing a calling pattern for salesmen to ensure systematic rather than haphazard coverage.

Rule Solid line in printing.

Run of paper (ROP) Instruction to a publisher indicating that no special position is sought for an advertisement, i.e. it can be placed in any convenient part of the advertising space of the publication. A lower charge is usually payable in such circumstances than where a specific position is demanded.

Run-of-week spot An arrangement whereby a TV contractor undertakes to transmit a commercial during a particular week but, since a discount is allowable, will not specify the exact time of transmission.

Rush   *See* Film rush.

S

Sack   Originally open-ended hessian container, but now more commonly made from multiwall paper or from plastic, used largely for bulk packaging of powders or granulated materials.

Sale or return   Colloquial term for practice whereby only goods resold are charged to a dealer, any unsold goods being returnable for full credit. *See* Consignment Selling, to which this is related.

Sales agency   Organization or person having the right to negotiate business with a third party on behalf of a principal, selling his goods or services according to a laid down agreement. The essence of an agency is that the agent drops out of the contract once it has been signed by the principal parties.

Sales aid   Any tangible element of sales promotion, leaflet, film projector or sample, which acts as a back-up to a salesman in presenting his proposition to a buyer.

Sales analysis   (1) Investigating company sales performances, especially in statistical form. (2) Published version of actual sales performance shown in tabulated form.

Sales approach   Positive proposition or theme adopted by salesmen to win a favourable reaction from prospects.

Sales barometer   Means of comparing the level of sales performance against preset standards.

Sales budget   Tabulation of anticipated accounting

figures covering sales revenue and direct selling costs, shown in predetermined divisions of time, products, territory or market segment. Used as a means of control by comparing actual with budgeted performance and taking remedial action, where possible, to restore any shortfalls.

Sales campaign Implementation of the selling strategy. Sometimes mounting a specific selling operation for a product, a market segment, or a geographical area, in isolation from the normal sales activity.

Sales conference Gathering, often annual, of all the personnel involved in selling, and often sales promotion, activities in a company to review past performance and examine targets, incentives, and techniques for the future.

Sales control Use of system or procedures to enable supervisory personnel to monitor the performance of the selling operation, particularly in relation to the field force, using predetermined aims or goals.

Sales costs Costs of field selling effort.

Sales feature Aspect of a product which can be shown as a customer benefit.

Sales force Group of salesmen, directed by a national or regional sales manager.

Sales forecasts Projections of likely sales, given certain defined criteria and making defined assumptions. Often based upon historical data. Not identical to sales targets which relate purely to the salesmen they concern.

Sales incentives (1) a) Financial incentives to salesmen by provision of commissions, prizes, bonuses, etc. b) Non-financial incentives such as award of status symbols. (2) Promotional devices and gifts offered to trade buyers, potential customers, or to distribution channels, in order to promote sales or extra selling effort.

Sales inquiry Request from sales prospect for sales literature or quotation. (Enquiry is a general term used for requests for non-sales information.)

127

Sales kit Sales presentation, communicational selling aids and administrative stationery and equipment carried by the salesman for the transaction of business.

Sales lead Piece of information or a contact which may ultimately lead to a sale being transacted. *See* Sales inquiry.

Sales literature Pamphlets, leaflets, point-of-sale showcards, etc. which give product information to potential customers.

Salesman/Saleslady (1) Retail sales staff in a store. (2) Employee of wholesale or manufacturing distributor calling upon retailers or other potential customers soliciting orders. *See* Sales representative.

Sales manager Executive responsible for sales force management, directly through field sales managers or through branch or area organization. Often also controls some internal sales service, which may or may not include transport, credit, repair, maintenance or other services.

Sales management Organization, direction, control, recruitment, training and motivation of the field selling effort within the planned marketing strategy.

Salesmanship Practice of informing and persuading persons or organizations of the value of a purchase and expressing that value in actual benefits unique to each prospect.

Sales manual Guide to operating instructions, terms of employment and policy document issued to salesmen as a supplement to sales training and supervision.

Sales meeting Gathering of salesmen usually led by a field supervisor, for a training session or for dissemination of information.

Sales mobility Indicates extent of ability and positive or negative attitude shown in responding to customers' requests for out-of-schedule visits.

Sales office manager Executive responsible for

managing the sales office and, in particular, ensuring that the necessary back-up is provided to the sales force in using company resources efficiently, thus exerting maximum persuasional effect upon customers.

Sales organization   Structure and distribution of the sales personnel, head and branch offices or warehouses and possibly shops, where company-operated. Can also be applied in same way to organization of sales staff in a mail order operation.

Sales organizer   *See* Portfolio.

Sales penetration   Extent to which total market potential has been realized, i.e. the proportion of people in that market who have become users or consumers of a product or service.

Sales planning   Determining sales objectives and selling activity quotas in an effort to achieve pre-set sales targets.

Sales platform   Main selling proposition upon which a particular campaign is to be based.

Sales policies   Company policies enjoined upon the sales force in order to promote uniform achievement of marketing objectives.

Sales potential   Share of a market that a company believes is achievable when its plans and strategies have been fully implemented.

Sales power   Measure of company strength in selling effort and achievement compared with that of competitors' equivalents.

Sales promotion   Any non-face-to-face activity concerned with the promotion of sales, but often taken also to include advertising. In consumer marketing, frequently used to denote any below-the-line advertising expenditure and having close connections with in-store merchandising.

Sales quota   Goal set for man, product, territory, or market segment in selling activity or sales performance terms. *See* Quota (2).

129

E

Sales records Collections of data relating to sales achieved by product category, geographical location, customer type, etc.

Sales representative Sales person usually associated with technical or professional selling, although often acknowledged as a facade created by sales people and their managers in an effort to embellish their function.

Sales research Study of field and office activities in an effort to discover means of improving sales force productivity.

Sales resistance Rational or irrational opposition to a buying proposition. Will either be dispelled by salesman effort or persist irrespective of how, or the extent to which, the proposition is presented.

Sales service All the productive, clerical and administrative facilities which are provided as a support to the activities of the sales force in order to service customer requirements.

Sales strategy Plan of the sales activities undertaken to achieve set objectives including territory targets, methods of selling, rates of calling and budgets; a subsection of established marketing strategy.

Sales targets Quantitative sales objectives set as a positive statement of company requirements as compared with sales forecasts which are related more to an objective assessment of anticipated events based upon external factors not within the company's control. *See* Sales Quota.

Sales territory Geographical area, market segment, or product group within which individual sales people are responsible for developing sales.

Sales tools Synonym for sales aids.

Sales volume Sales achievement expressed in quantitative, physical or volume terms.

Same size Instruction to a printer or production house

to reproduce an original in the same size. Commonly abbreviated 'SS'.

Sample (1) Representative item or portion used by salesmen to assist in convincing buyers of product's quality. (2) Representative microcosm of the entire population or universe taken to represent the characteristics of the whole. Accuracy of resultant information may be calculated according to sample size and sampling technique used.

Sample case Mobile container used, for instance, by salesmen for carriage, protection and demonstration of samples of their company's products.

Sampling error (1) Bias in one or more aspects of a sampling frame. (2) Standard error. *See* Deviation. *See also* Normal distribution.

Sampling frame Control data for research study; specifies parameters and structure for each sample.

Sampling offers Invitations by manufacturers to potential customers to 'try' the product by taking a free sample or lower-priced trial pack.

Sampling point Geographical location convenient for contacting a predetermined cluster of informants.

Saturation campaign Intensive use of mass media in a single campaign.

Saturation point Level at which any further expansion of distribution in a market is unlikely to be achieved and where further sales are restricted to the potential arising from replacement needs or population growth.

Scamp Rough design of layout of advertisement or other promotional material.

Script Text of a commercial film or broadcast.

Schedule *See* Advertising schedule.

Scheme advertising Advertising normally of a below-the-line character. *See* Theme advertising.

Screening Procedure by which new or modified product ideas are assessed in a methodical way against key factors for success. Products not meeting the essential criteria are thus eliminated at an early stage in their development. This is a discipline which should be imposed early on in the concept development stage in order to eliminate unnecessary wastage of resources on ideas which are unlikely to be successful.

Seasonal concentration Limiting sales or promotional campaigns to appropriate segments of the year.

Seasonal discount Discount offered by media owners to encourage business during what are considered to be slack periods in the year.

Seasonal rate Rates in advertising which vary according to the time of year.

Secondary coverage Area in which reception of radio or television channel is subject to variation; usually the area concerned is catered for by another channel but is within the outer area of another. *See* Overlap.

Secondary readership Indicates readership of a publication by location, e.g. by the members of a household whose head buys the publication or by people in an organization which subscribes to it, sometimes referred to as 'pass-on readership'.

Second generation product Product which evolves from one already on the market and eventually supersedes it. Term commonly used in areas of rapid technological development, e.g. electronics.

Segmentation Breakdown of a market into discrete and identifiable elements, each of which may have its own special requirements of a product and each of which is likely to exhibit different habits affecting its exposure to advertising media. Other marketing factors such as optimum price, quality, packaging and distribution are likely to differ as between one segment and another.

Typical breakdowns are based upon age, social standing, income, sex, geographical location, leisure pursuits.

Selective positioning Choice and continuity of a special position within a type of advertising medium, aimed at a specific target audience.

Selective selling Selling which is confined to those customers and prospects which satisfy a minimum standard of performance or some other limiting factor. Formerly a common practice for the distribution of speciality products but breaking down as mass marketing techniques are more widely exploited. *See* Exclusive agency agreement.

Self-liquidating offer Special offer (or gift) made available to purchasers of a product, and designed to yield sufficient revenue to defray the cost of the offer and also perhaps reduce the promotional costs involved.

Self-mailer Direct mail piece that can be posted without envelope or wrapper; a form of postcard.

Self-service store Retail outlet where customers help themselves to prepriced goods from shelves or other displays, and pay for their purchases at suitably located cash tills or in total upon departure. *See* Checkout.

Sellers' market Excess of demand over supply creating market imbalance and making sales effort less obligatory on the part of suppliers. *See* Buyers' market.

Selling Process of persuasion leading to a continuing trading arrangement, initiated and perpetuated at either a personal or impersonal level but commonly confined to oral representation supported by visual aids.

Selling agent Salesman representing an organization but not necessarily on the organization's payroll. *See* Commission.

Semantic differential Choice from an arrangement of preselected phrases to enable informant to register one with the closest affinity to his/her own opinion. Often expressed in a complete spectrum, e.g. excellent to poor, from which respondent chooses the description most nearly corresponding with his/her own views.

Seminar Meeting set up for the dissemination of knowledge in which a 'leader' discusses a subject with his audience rather than expounding it. Frequently a small and informal grouping in UK but can be organized on a large scale of conference proportions.

Semi-solus Advertisement which appears on a page containing another advertisement but which is not positioned adjacent to it.

Semi-structured Research conducted by interviewer with guidelines but in which certain key questions may need to be answered.

Sentence completion Establishing attitudes or opinions by providing incomplete questions that the respondent may answer in any fashion he/she chooses. Often portrays the irrational areas of motivation that are difficult to elicit and summarize from a conventional interviewing situation.

Sequential Taking events one at a time in an orderly fashion, usually according to some agreed procedure.

Series discount Discount given by advertising media owner in consideration of an undertaking by an advertiser to book a series of insertions within a given minimum number of issues.

Service department Part of an organization concerned with providing after-sales service to customers; frequently involved with the handling of complaints which require tactful replacement or rectification to avoid temporary or permanent loss of goodwill.

Service fee Charge made, usually on a predetermined annual basis, by an advertising or public relations agency for the service it provides. Increasingly used instead of, or in addition to, the earlier convention of commission income. *See* Commission (3).

Service industries   Suppliers of services not directly involved with manufacturing, e.g. travel, entertainment, health, insurance, professional and personal treatment.

Set solid   Lines of type which are set close up to one another, without any spacing.

Sheet (prefixed 4, 8, 16, 32, etc.)   Means of describing the dimensions of a poster based on multiples of a double crown, i.e. a double sheet poster measuring 30 ins × 20 ins. Therefore, a four sheet poster would measure 60 ins × 40 ins.

Shelf life   Limit of time during which a product may be stored on a retailer's shelves before natural deterioration will render it unfit for sale. *See* Date coding.

Shell scheme   Standard design of individual booth provided by the organizer of an exhibition.

Shipping note   Delivery note used by exporters to notify the docks of an intended consignment specifying the vessel and sailing date.

Shooting   Synonym for filming in colloquial usage.

Shooting script   Schedule of activities in film making which relates each part of a script to the accompanying visual and sound effect.

Shoplifting   Stealing from retail stores with intention to evade payment for them leading to stock 'shrinkages'.

Shopping centres   Urban marketing developments planned and operated under local government regulation in UK and providing for a full representation of shopping facilities in the interests of the local community.

Short rate   Difference between the rate paid by an advertiser at the end of a period between the actual number of lines taken up by advertising in a publication and the estimated lines upon which an original quotation was based.

Showcase Cabinet made of glass or clear plastic to display products protected against deterioration and pilferage. Though extensively used at point-of-sale, showcases are widely used at public and private exhibitions, e.g. hotel foyers, when an indication will be given of where displayed articles may be purchased.

Shrink wrapping Enclosure of goods in a transparent film of plastic which is 'shrunk' onto the goods by the application of heat. Often used as an alternative to an outer container where protection is not a key factor but display is. Used especially for dispensing fresh foodstuffs in self-service stores and supermarkets. *See* Blister pack.

Sight draft Bill of exchange payable on sight.

Signals, buying Indication of a prospect's willingness to make a purchase perceived by a salesman as the preliminary to the use of closing techniques.

Significance (1) Generally used to suggest relevance. (2) Statistical term with similar meaning but with more precise implication. Statistical tests are used to establish the significance level, e.g. T-tests (taking differences between average values) and Chi-tests (testing differences between distributions).

Silent salesman Point-of-sale material embodying display and especially attention-getting contents used as a merchandising technique. Is also often used to describe packaging.

Silk screening Method of printing by which ink is forced through a fine mesh on which have been superimposed opaque areas, representing the reverse of the design, through which ink will not pass. Much used in the production of high quality point-of-sale material.

Simulation Representation of one system by means of

another. In particular, the representation of physical performance by computers, either equipment or models, to facilitate the study of such systems or phenomena to train operators etc. (BS 3527).

Single column centimetre (scc) Standard unit of measurement for print advertisements; one centimetre in a column. *See* Single column inch.

Single column inch (sci) Obsolescent measurement in newspapers and magazines in UK, based upon the depth of type matter contained in a single column. *See* Single column centimetre.

Single source Information or data received or compiled from one origin alone, most often in connection with a research study.

Situation report Report on the current situation or circumstances; often shortened to . . . sitrep.

Sixteen sheet Most popular size of poster consisting of eight double crown sizes. *See* Double crown.

Skewness Distribution of data which differs from a normal distribution in that the mean and the mode are located at different points.

Skimming price Price aimed at appealing to higher income groups. *See* Penetration pricing.

Sleeper effect Studies which have shown that, even after the purely factual information within it has been forgotten, attitudes may still have shifted in favour of an advertisement, indicating that an attitude change has been effected. This is known as the sleeper effect.

Slogan Catchwords, phrase or sentence associated with a product or company, encapsulating a particularly pertinent selling point in a succinct and sometimes entertaining fashion.

Small order problem Arises from receipt of orders of insufficient unit value to justify handling; such a problem can be overcome by using dropshipment via intermediary stockists, by making such orders subject to deposit of cash price in advance of delivery or by fixing a minimum order size/value.

Socio-economic groups   Breakdown of population into sections to represent main subsections of a community according to selected economic and social criteria. The groups are designated by a letter series, namely, A, B, C1, C2, D, E, in which A and B represent the minority of higher income receivers in the scale, D and E the lower skilled, lower earners and C1 and C2 occupying a position midway between these extremes. Introduced by the IPA in 1962, as an aid to media distribution analysis, the scale has been the subject of wide contention, since it is felt to be inadequate to reflect the facts of market segmentation in an era of rapid social changes. On the other hand, complex problems of social measurement are involved in any attempt to set up any superior alternative.

Sod's law   Obtuse incongruity of inanimate objects, e.g. the door to a telephone booth will always seem to be on the opposite side to one's approach.

Soft selling   Couching the selling message in a subtle or oblique way, as against a blatant or hard selling approach. Sometimes known as 'low pressure selling'.

Sole trader   One-man trading concern, representing the simplest and earliest form of business organization.

Solus position   Position of isolation (i.e. separated from any immediate, especially competitive, announcements) of a poster or press advertisement, for instance.

Sound track   Narrow area running alongside the film which carries the sound recording. Is often used to refer to the actual sound recording itself.

Space buyer   *See* Media buyer.

Span of control Breadth of control, measured in numbers of personnel and the rigour of their duties, which a manager or executive may supervise effectively.

Speciality salesman Used in connection with sales personnel who are usually confined to one product or at most a limited range of products and frequently where there is a once-only selling opportunity or at least little likelihood of a repeat sale in the immediate future.

Special position Insertion of an advertisement in what is regarded as a distinctive position in a publication, e.g. outside or inside covers, or facing matter. Such a selection frequently involves a higher charge being made to the advertiser and advance action on his part to secure it.

Specification In marketing, this relates to the specified characteristics and performance required of a product, expressed in quantitative as well as qualitative terms. In production terms, specification is a schedule of parts or a list of ingredients from which a product is manufactured.

Specific offer Precise proposition by the seller with a view to securing a contract to use or purchase a product or service.

Spectacular (1) Large, outdoor, electrically illuminated sign. (2) Unusual direct mail piece. (3) Elaborate special TV programme, irregularly scheduled.

Split credit sales Division of credit between salesmen for business obtained, where orders are secured from one sales territory but delivery is required on another. The arrangement may also apply to orders booked via a head or branch office which are then delivered in one or more sales territories; such apportionment assists in the compilation of sales statistics and comparisons as well as the payment of appropriate commissions to the salesmen concerned.

Split run When the identical publication is printed and distributed in two or more separate production runs and deliveries to facilitate the insertion of different advertisements in each part run. The arrangement is often used to compare the measured effects of alternative pieces of advertising copy.

Sponsored book Book specially produced for an organization which undertakes to meet all or most of the production cost to the publisher, such publications being produced for public relations' purposes.

Sponsored events In marketing, part of a public relations programme to emphasize the name of an organization or product in a favourable light by paying all or some of the costs of a public sport or spectacle, e.g. cricket or motor-racing. The technique can be used in relation to any event which is likely to be patronized or otherwise come to the attention of the particular public the organization desires to influence.

Spot Single television advertisement appearance.

Spot lengths Standard times for television commercials, e.g. 7, 15, 30, 45 and 60 seconds; 30 seconds being the base time. *See* Timelength.

Spread traffic *See* Page traffic.

Stand out test In consumer goods marketing, a package on shelf store test to determine how well the designed package shows up when compared with competitive offerings in close proximity and display.

Stamp trading Incentive vouchers, usually in the form of stamps, issued by retailers in relation to value of purchases to encourage trading loyalty; stamps may later be redeemed for cash (a legal requirement), or goods chosen by the consumer from a catalogue and collected from a stocking and display point. The practice has been outlawed in N. America where it was found to be subject to abuse.

Standard deviation *See* Deviation (standard).

Standard error Measurement of accuracy of statistical

measurements of sample. Expressed in two dimensions; the parameters of accuracy and the confidence level at which the study was undertaken.

Standard industrial classification (SIC) Comprehensive listing and coding of industries and services by the UK Government's Central Statistical Office (Central Office of Information), and published by Her Majesty's Stationery Office (HMSO).

Standardized sales presentation Prepared sales sequence following a definite course of action developed by experienced sales personnel for the benefit of new or inexperienced recruits.

Starch ratings Method of measuring advertisement effectiveness in the USA. *See* Reading and noting.

Statement Financial document showing net total of outstanding accounts owing to the seller by the buyer after taking into consideration all due allowances and payments received. Usually but not always a monthly issue.

Static market Market which has a pattern over time substantially free from fluctuations, particularly of volume.

Status inquiry Form of checking upon the credit worthiness of a prospective customer, sometimes known as 'credit rating'.

Status symbol (1) Non-financial incentives offered to salesmen. (2) Prestigeous products bought more for purposes of ostentation than for their utility; buyers may or may not make extensive use of such purchases.

Statute of Limitations UK legislation, fixing period within which outstanding debts may be legally collected: outside such period the indebtedness lapses.

Stereotype Printing plate cast in one piece from a matrix or mould.

Sterling area Group of countries using the British

pound as a reserve currency, agreeing to permit free transfer of funds amongst members and to operate joint control over exchanges of sterling area currencies for other external currencies.

Sticker Label, poster or other printed sheet intended for sticking on window, letter, envelope or other medium for display purposes.

Still Single frame printed from photograph used in a continuous film. Generally refers to a photograph rather than the movie-film as such.

Stimulus Initiating step or incentive intended to provoke a predictable response.

Stockist Stockholder of a specific range of goods for sale on behalf of a particular supplier.

Stop motion Photographic technique for animating inanimate objects.

Store demonstration Public demonstration of machines, product, or equipment held in a store.

Storyboard Sequence of sketches designed to show the main elements of television or cinema commercial.

Strategic planning *See* Corporate planning.

Stratification Structuring requirements or procedure laid down within a research survey questionnaire for the uniform control of interviews in such a way as to permit reliable summaries and comparisons of results to be drawn up.

Strengths and weaknesses Used to categorize elements and characteristics of products or organizations to assess positive and negative features, particularly for competitive comparisons.

Stuffer Piece of publicity matter intended for general distribution with other material such as outgoing mail or goods, e.g. 'envelope stuffer'.

Subliminal projection Delivery of an advertising

message below receiver's level of awareness, but which registers in the subconscious. May be visual or audio or both. The use of subliminal advertising is illegal in the UK and a number of other countries where it is not regarded as a fair means of exercising persuasive influence.

Subsample   Subsection of a sample.

Subscribed circulation   The part of a publisher's circulation which is paid for, as opposed to being distributed free of charge. *See* Controlled circulation.

Suggestion selling   Presenting selling arguments by suggestion, whereby the prospect may feel he has arrived at a conclusion (favourable to the selling agent) as a result of his own persuasions.

Supermarket   (1) Self-service store of over 2000 square feet and having three or more check-out points, mostly having a wide range of fast-moving merchandise, including a high proportion of foodstuffs, usually at premium prices. (2) Site where many traders operate their business on their own account under the same roof.

Superstore   *See* Hypermarket.

Supplement   Special feature section of a publication.

Survey   Study based on sampling techniques.

Symbol   Distinctive sign or graphic design denoting a company or product. Often a pictorial presentation of a company or product name. *See* Logotype.

Syndicated   Multiclient project with no one client exercising exclusive rights.

Synergy   Term used to identify the condition where the combined effect of two or more courses of action is greater than the sum of the individual parts. In marketing, frequently applied to the measure of overall effectiveness through the co-ordinated operation of the many elements comprising the marketing mix.

143

T

Tabloid   Newspaper with a small page area.

Tabulation   Putting data into tables, usually of a numerical order.

Tachistoscope   In advertising research, a projection device used to measure the thresholds at which the features of an advertisement are registered. Is also used for measuring visual impact of an advertisement when exposed for only a short time.

Tallyman   Collection agent for loan/insurance companies.

Target weights   Used for weighting advertising expenditure; a means of varying expenditure according to the influence of demographic factors. *See* Weighting.

Task method   Means of calculating the budget for an advertising campaign by relating it to the objective(s) to be achieved, rather than by using any given amount of money arrived at in a more arbitrary fashion.

Tax incidence   Point where ultimate tax burden is located.

Tax, Turnover   Tax levied as the proportion of the price of a commodity at each level of distribution. Commonly known as VAT (value added tax).

Tear sheet   Press advertisement torn from a newspaper or periodical and sent to an advertiser as evidence of its publication. *See* Voucher.

Teaser   Advertisement which by withholding information about the product and/or sponsor, is designed to arouse widespread attention through the operation of curiosity. Often takes the form of a poster or series of posters.

Technical press   Periodicals dealing with technical subjects. Usually grouped together as 'trade & technical', referring in effect to all publications directed to a non-consumer public.

Telephone answering service   Mechanical or manual servicing of calls or inquiries through the telephone network.

Telephone selling   Selling operation in which the telephone is used to contact potential customers, and to solicit orders without any personal call upon customers' premises.

Television consumer audit   Organization of a sample of viewers who report findings and thus enable television impact on population to be measured.

Temporary exports   Samples or exhibits required to be re-imported within an agreed period of time.

Tender   Offer to supply goods or services at a price: usually a detailed document outlining all the conditions which would relate to any ensuing contract. Commonly associated with Government contracts for building, construction service or period supplies.

Terminal markets   Markets dealing in futures where dealers and importers have the opportunity to buy supplies at currently ruling prices. Especially common in the sale of agricultural products, e.g. wool, but also used for many other basic commodities, e.g. metals.

Terms of trade   Ratio of index of export prices to index of import prices, showing a relationship for comparison purposes between levels of prices at home and overseas.

Tertiary readership   Indicates readership of a publication seen casually during or while waiting for some other activity, normally outside the home, e.g. at hairdressers or surgery.

Test close   Requesting the buyer to place an order for the purpose of establishing the extent to which he is ready to buy and thus enabling the interview to be conducted economically.

Test marketing   Method of testing a marketing plan on a limited scale, simulating as nearly as possible all the factors involved in a national campaign; usually carried out in a restricted but representative location, often a particular TV region. This procedure enables a marketing company to obtain an indication of likely market acceptance without the full commitment and expense of a national launch. It also exposes the product and the plan to competitors, and consequently the results of the test can seldom be regarded as absolutely conclusive.

Testimonial advertisement   Piece of promotion which uses the implied or explicit patronage of a product by a well-known person, or organization. *See* Personality promotions.

Tetra pack   Four-sided container, usually constructed from waxed paper and designed for dispensing liquids, e.g. milk, frequently in portions for individual serving.

Text   Solid typematter as distinct from headlines.

Theme advertising   Advertising, normally of an above-the-line character. *See* Scheme advertising.

Threshold goals   Minimum level of achievement acceptable.

Throw-away   *See* Give-away.

Thumbnail   Miniature sketch.

Tied loan   Loan from one country to another but conditional on the borrower buying specified goods or services to the value concerned from the lender country.

Timelength   Time of a commercial spot in television or radio. *See* Spot lengths.

Times 1000   Annual publication ranking the top 1000 British companies by sales turnover, profitability and capital employed. Also includes details of European, American and Japanese companies, operating in the UK.

Tip   Optional gratuity; commonly included in the overall charge and characterized as a service charge. Familiar mostly in service industries, e.g. hotels and catering.

Title or Credit title   List of executives and performers in a television or film programme.

Tote system   Service offered by British Rail involving a tote bin specially designed for the transport of goods in bulk. Particularly applies to movement of materials in granular, powder or liquid form.

Trade Descriptions Act, 1968 and 1972   UK law limiting the freedom of companies to describe their products or their trading activities. Is administered by the Department of Weights and Measures through a national inspectorate and replaces the Merchandise Marks Acts of 1887 and 1957.

Trade fairs   Fairs held in a selected national market to show and promote goods made in another country or made under licence or other arrangements in the country concerned.

Trade mark   Mark used in relation to goods so as to indicate a connection in the course of trade between the goods and the proprietor or registered supplier. Registration under the appropriate Act provides exclusive right of usage.

Trade press   Strictly referring to periodicals dealing with particular trades. *See* Technical press.

Trade price   Discounted price for the benefit of another in a trading position and not usually open to a consumer.

Trade setting   Typesetting by a trade house on direct instructions from a client or agency, usually working to tight specifications and resulting in higher quality output. Compare Paper setting.

Trading down   Selling at low prices to achieve high volume; most usually involves lower grade or deteriorated products, where the price structure will permit such a strategy. *See* Trading up.

Trading stamps   *See* Stamp trading.

Trading up   Selling at high prices supported by a high level of service in order to secure exclusive custom and high profit ratios. *See* Trading down.

Traffic   (1) Progressing and scheduling of activities in an advertising agency to ensure events take place on time and are completed according to requirement. (2) Pattern of movement of customers in a store, observed or induced.

Traffic count   Count of persons (or vehicles) passing a particular point during a specified period of time.

Tramp steamer   Independent vessel available for the carriage of any type of goods.

Transfer prices   Special prices charged to an associated company carrying no profit and usually making no allowance for marketing costs, e.g. delivery. *See* Reciprocal trading.

Transport advertising   Special form of poster advertising sited on or inside buses, main line and Tube railway trains, or other forms of transportation, e.g. taxi-cabs and trucks. Also refers to posters exhibited at railway stations, bus stops, airline terminals, seaports and the like.

Trans-shipment   Goods transferred to another vessel to complete the journey to their ultimate destination. A means of diversion from main transport lines to more isolated places.

Travellers' cheques   Personalized credit forms issued by banks, usually for overseas travel and redeemed by signature. Replaceable in the event of loss, they reduce the necessity for holding large amounts of currency which involves greater risk of loss.

Travelling exhibition   Exhibition designed to be fully mobile. May be generally mobile on a planned circuit, e.g. by road, or confined to a rail or sea network, e.g. exhibition train or ship.

Treasury bill Bill of exchange issued by the British Government and payable within three months. Holding is mainly confined to the large joint stock banks in connection with fiscal controls within the economy, but other finance houses especially the building societies, for example, may purchase them as a good form of liquid reserve.

Treatment Sequential descriptive document in film making, giving a detailed outline of the form a film is likely to take. Used generally with same meaning in relation to any form of planned communication.

Trend analysis Extrapolation of historical figures for the purpose of studying their significance.

Triad Test of selection, usually from three products offered to informant – one varied in some way from the other two – with an invitation to choose the one preferred.

Trial close Attempt by salesman to close an interview or assess the direction in which it is progressing by asking specifically or even indirectly for the order before the proposition or demonstration has been completed. *See* Test close.

Trial order Small order, placed specifically to judge the value or quality of a proposition, prior to placing a substantial order or sequence of orders.

T-Test Statistical test to measure differences between two average values.

Tube Cylindrical pack made from soft metal, e.g. for toothpaste, rigid metal, e.g. for cigars, plastics, e.g. for cosmetics, or fibreboard, e.g. for maps.

Tube cards Advertisements inside railway compartments, particularly associated with Greater London Tube train network.

Turnover (1) Total period sales figure of a business or organization, expressed by value or volume but usually the former. (2) In recruitment, the measure of the mobility of staff in an organization.

Turnover, rate of Number of times the average value of stock is sold during a period. Formula for calculation:

$$\frac{\text{value of sales at cost}}{\text{Average stock at cost}} \times 100$$

Turnover of salesman Number of salesmen leaving employment of a company during a specific period of time, usually expressed as a percentage of the sales force.

TVR Television rating; indicates coverage of target audiences by individual programes or advertisements on commercial televison. *See* Rating.

Two-colour Number of colours used in printing an advertisement or publication. Usually black plus one other.

Type Characters made of metal or plastics and used in printing.

Type area Space which is available on a page in a publication for printing.

Typeface *See* Face.

Typographer Person, frequently but not always an employee of an advertising agency, who produces type layouts or type markups, i.e. accurate specifications from which a printer can carry out typesetting.

Typological analysis Combination of households into 'generic' classifications. The aim is to establish distinct profiles for given families or households.

U

Unilateral One-sided proposition, decision, or agreement.

Unique selling proposition (USP) Product benefit

which can be regarded as unique as a primary selling argument.

Unit pack Pack which contains only one product or unit.

Universe Population (or subsection of the population) from which a research sample is drawn.

Unloading Disposing of goods in a market at a low or concessionary price. *See* Dumping.

Upper case Capital letters in printing or typescript. *See* Lower case.

Upset price Lowest price at which negotiations can begin. Often used in auctioneering as the price from which bidding is invited.

Usage pull Technique ascribed to Rosser Reeves in USA, to discern the proportionate change in usage of a product as between those who are familiar with its advertising and those who are not.

Usury Generic term for the lending of money in return for payment of interest, usually at a fixed rate of interest regardless of the rate of repayment.

Utility (1) Psychological satisfaction derived from a purchase – the converse of the modern use of the term as defined in (2) below. (2) Sufficient to perform a prescribed function without elaboration. Utility goods prevail during emergency conditions, e.g. war.

V

Vacillating customer Customer unwilling, or unable, to determine own needs when presented with positive proposition.

Value added tax Tax levied on a product at each stage of manufacture or distribution related directly to the estimated or actual increase in sales value. Successor to purchase taxes in UK. *See* Turnover tax.

Value analysis Examination of every constituent of a product to ensure that its cost is no greater than is necessary to carry out its function. Sometimes referred to as value engineering.

Valued impressions per pound (VIP) (1) Number of readers divided by the advertising rate. The VIP index shows how many readers are bought for a given sum of money. (2) Weighted media target multiplied by media weight and divided by cost of advertisement.

Value judgement Subjective expression of opinion unsupported by fact or available data.

Variable costs Accounting term for costs that vary directly with output, as opposed to fixed costs.

Variance (1) Management accounting term indicating the difference between a budgeted item and its actual cost or performance. (2) Statistical term for the arithmetic mean of the square deviations of the values from the mean. (3) In a dispute, disagreement between executives on questions of policy or strategy.

Vehicle Particular publication or channel used to carry advertising message.

Vending machine Purely automatic dispensing of solid or liquid products on insertion of specified coinage. Also used for services, e.g. laundering. *See* Robot salesmen.

Vertical circulation Business publication edited for persons at all levels in a specific industry or profession, e.g. *British Printer*. *See* Horizontal publication.

Vertical integration (1) Refers to the merging of companies producing different things but contributing to the same ultimate product, e.g. between a car seats producer and a windscreens manufacturer. (2) Company operating at more than one level in channels of distribution, typically as both manufacturer and distributor, e.g. Boots the Chemists.

Vested interest Material involvement of a person or organization in the outcome of a venture or the maintenance of the status quo.

Video tape recording (VTR) Pictures and sound recorded magnetically on tape which can then be reproduced upon a cathode ray tube. Often used for television commercials and programmes but also suitable for many forms of instructional training and evaluation of personnel.

Vinylite Plastic matrix.

Visiting cards Business cards identifying caller usually confined to name and organization but may also include nature of business and occasionally a sales promotion message.

Visual Drawing or illustration of an advertisement or other piece of promotional material, finished to an adequate standard for presentation to a client. *See* Layout.

Visualizer Designer responsible for producing visual ideas for the interpretation and execution of an advertising brief. Usually, but not necessarily, an employee of an advertising agency.

Voice over Narration with narrator not on screen, possibly with still photograph, used for commercials.

Voluntary chain or group Association of independent traders using collective power for purchasing, promotional and development purposes. A chain usually confines its membership to retail buyers while a voluntary group is based upon a wholesaler in association with a group of retailers.

Voluntary controls (advertising) System of selfcontrol adopted by UK advertising practitioners to ensure that advertisements conform to a defined code of practice. *See* ASA and Codes of Practice.

Voucher   Free copy of a periodical sent to an advertiser or agency as evidence of an advertisement having been published. *See* Tear Sheet.

Voyage charter   Scheduled cruise to a certain destination and back, usually for specified societies and associations under prescribed trading arrangements which permit lower unit prices to be charged.

W

Warehouse   Storage site for finished goods. Provides local availability prior to sale.

Waste circulation   Parts of a circulation which are of no value to the advertiser but which he nevertheless has to pay for in his campaign.

Web-offset   Method of offset-litho printing in which paper is fed into the press from a reel as compared with a sheet feed.

Weighting   Varying particular information inputs according to known but different standards so as to provide for more realistic results.

Whole plate   *See* Full plate.

Wholesaler   Intermediary between the retailer and manufacturer. Usually buys goods in quantity at a discount and sells them in small batches at higher unit prices. An important facility for distribution of goods of smaller manufacturers, especially in non-urban areas, but also has a high utility in cities for urgently required immediate supplies.

Window dressing   (1) Displaying goods in a shop window to best advantage to attract custom. *See* Display. (2) Arranging goods or presentation in such a way as to impress another party; sometimes used to describe an artificial situation with the intention to mislead.

Window shopping Visiting shops without an immediate intention or inclination to buy.

Workload schedule Forward plan of work for executive and sales personnel.

Write-off Reducing the value of an asset to zero either for tax benefit, trading advantage, or to reflect its true market value. Often leads to its disposal.

X

X (X bar) Statistical symbol for average.

Y

Year books *See* Annuals.

Yield Profit or revenue attributable to a product or company's shares. May be expressed in absolute or relative terms.

Z

Z chart A diagram charting values over a period (frequently one year) and showing simultaneously cumulative totals and the moving averages. It normally takes a Z shape, hence its title, and is of use in clarifying the trends present in the data displayed. A main feature of Interfirm comparisons, for example.

Zone Any territorial area in which for the time being marketing operations are confined.

Zoom

Zoom   Fast action of continuous change in focal length in a special lens giving the impression that the television or film camera has moved rapidly towards the object being focused, or vice versa when used in reverse.